W9-AFM-405

SECOND ESSAYS ON LITERATURE

SECOND ESSAYS ON LITERATURE

by

EDWARD SHANKS

Essay Index Reprint Series

BOOKS FOR LIBRARIES PRESS
FREEPORT, NEW YORK

First Published 1927
Reprinted 1968

LIBRARY OF CONGRESS CATALOG CARD NUMBER:
68-20334
PRINTED IN THE UNITED STATES OF AMERICA

To

T. Michael Pope

Preface

When, about three years ago, I published my first series of essays on literature, I asked that they might be taken as attempts to discover some sort of a critical method. What this method should be now seems a little clearer to me, and perhaps I may be allowed to say a few more words upon it, more especially since even the kindest of my reviewers then found fault with me upon a point of method in a manner which I thought not quite fair.

They complained of a lack of enthusiastic appreciation, of a certain chilliness of treatment, and in particular that I made no attempt to fire any one to read the authors of whom I was writing. But this, I think now, though then I realised it only unconsciously, was no part of my intention. That was purely analytical, theoretic, and, above all, descriptive. Perhaps the greatest, certainly the most delightful, critics are those who can communicate their own pleasure in masterpieces. But there is surely a place for the critic who states quite coolly, and the more coolly the better, what a masterpiece seems to him to be.

He is likely enough to give a false description. But, one might almost affirm, in criticism it does not matter so much what we say, so long as we all say different things. There is here no absolute truth, not even that working approximation to it which serves us well enough in the other activities of life. There is only a number of opinions, of differing but hardly estimable values. A poem is in the long run what it is thought to be: the successful critic is he who can discern and state in words what in the long run, a term covering much more than a single generation, it will be thought to be.

Among these opinions one which merely states and analyses the character of a work of literature, whatever may be its inaccuracies, at least provides a fixed point from which to reckon. It may even provide a corrective on those occasions when enthusiasm makes a misleading picture of its subject.

This, then, in ideal terms, has been my intention, to make as it were a map of some part of modern literature. And by modern literature I mean not only contemporary authors but also those authors of other times in whom our own time finds for itself a new and a special significance. It is a changing body, bearing some resemblance to an assembly the members of which are appointed on different qualifications. Living writers figure in it out of proportion to their eternal value; dead writers enter it when the spirit of the time finds a use for them. It is by no means the whole of literature but it constitutes the atmosphere of thought and feeling which we breathe and in which we live our daily lives.

Like the atmosphere, it is difficult to apprehend as a concrete thing, and also, like the atmosphere, it is the battle-ground of violent and unpredictable disturbances. Fortunately, we are growing a little wiser in this as in the literal form of meteorology. When his admirers begin to grow a little weary of a great new French novelist, the advent of a great new Italian dramatist does not take us altogether by surprise. It would be absurd to pretend that these essays, or those in my previous book, are deliberately planned instalments of a complete system of meteorology. Both inclusions and omissions have been dictated by circumstances which would make any such plan impossible. But they are studies of patches taken here and there in one immense field always with the intention of making clear, if disputable, pictures of authors who are still alive in our contemporary world of thought and feeling.

I should add that of the essays in the present collection, nine were first printed in the *London Mercury*, and one each in the *Quarterly Review* and the *Illustrated Review*, and that I am indebted to the editors of these periodicals.

E. S.

Contents

Mr. Rudyard Kipling

It does not happen very often in English literature that the political opinions of a writer interfere with critical judgment of his work. Even at the beginning of last century, when the fear of all new things was powerfully aided by the fear of a particular new thing across the Channel which would be physically disagreeable if it ever came to England —even then the persecution of literary radicals seemed a little unnatural and a little absurd. Since then the question cannot be said to have arisen until the appearance of Mr. Rudyard Kipling. Tennyson wrote a good many poems on public subjects ; but it would be hard to conceive of opinion as to his poetic merits being moved by them, either one way or the other. Browning wrote a sonnet called *Why I am a Liberal* ; but do many readers know what precisely were the reasons he gave ? Morris preached Socialism ; and his work in all kinds was acutely appreciated by the rich, and in many kinds reserved for them alone. In truth, as a rule, the English keep their enjoyment of literature and their interest in politics in separate compartments ; and the political ideas of a poet or a novelist very rarely seem to them to be a genuine or an important part of the man himself.

With Mr. Kipling, however, it is altogether different. Since the height of his first fame he has been held to be a political figure ; and political points of view are almost always evident in critical considerations of his work, whether admiring or adverse. Mr. Kipling, so far I know, never has complained and, it may be suspected, never would complain of this. If it gets him severe and obstinate opponents, it also gets him enthusiastic admirers. Irish Nationalists sometimes unjustly transfer their angry contempt of such lines as :—

> " We know the war prepared
> On every peaceful home,
> We know the hells declared
> For such as serve not Rome,"

to everything which has been written by the same author. It is a regrettable thing : it obscures judgment. And yet, perhaps, were he too a critic of literature, Mr. Kipling's sympathies, so far as the principle of the thing goes, might very well be more with these than with those who regret alike the provocation and its result. He does not keep politics and literature in water-tight compartments. Politics is really his ruling and most permanent interest. In the whole-heartedness with which he takes a side, preaching both its general doctrines and its particular manœuvres, in the earnestness with which he publicly admonishes the entire nation on its own public affairs, we must find a comparison for him, if anywhere, abroad, for there is none to be found at home. His position, that is to say, in his writings, must be compared with the position of Hugo in France or of d'Annunzio in Italy—in his writings only, it must be confessed. The English nation has made something of a concession in taking so seriously his utterances on public matters. It might not have made the further concession which would have been necessary if he had definitely undertaken the day-to-day handling of day-to-day politics. Yet there was a time when he was almost himself a symbol rather than a creator or celebrator of symbols, just as d'Annunzio was the symbol of Italy's movement into the War.

Mr. Kipling's sudden and amazing upward rush into fame, over thirty years ago, coincided with the beginning of a period of English history which attained a melancholy culmination in the South African War. He came from India, both by birth and by early employment—employment during years which must have been decisive in forming a mind so precociously developed and since then so little open to change. He came to England from India with this at least definitely settled in his thoughts that (I am expressing it as mildly as possible) Liberal opinions on the treatment of subject races were in several particulars much mistaken. The conviction sprang by no means from a mere self-complacent belief in the superiority of the white race or from mere contempt for the "nigger." It sprang from a genuine love of efficiency and order. Mr. Kipling saw the English ruling India, as he thought, efficiently. He was far from despising the native races of India ; it is even fair to say that he loved them ; but he saw in their subordination a necessary principle of order, which ought not to produce shame. Even in that gentle book *Kim*, the country-bred boy, who has spent most of his life as a native, is made to assert his superiority as a Sahib over the Bengali, Hurree Chunder Mookerjee, who is his departmental superior. Kim does not much like doing it, but he knows it is the duty of his blood, and he does it, and is applauded, while the Babu acquiesces. Nowhere else, I think, has Mr. Kipling quite so clearly expressed in the abstract his doctrine that the white race must be the ruling race. And in this instance he emphasises his belief that the white race rules because, as a race, it is the most competent. The general principle must override exceptions—for he evinces anything but contempt for the Babu.

It is not my business to discuss here the value of these ideas. The point is that Mr. Kipling, fully possessed of them, brought them to an England which was fully ready for them. Those were the days when songs were sung with such refrains as " Paint another red patch on the map "; and the opinion was generally held that there were still a good many parts of the globe which could be ruled more efficiently by the English than by their own inhabitants. Those were the days when the young Cecil Rhodes made the first of his grandiose wills, leaving all his fortune (not then very great) for the foundation of a secret society which was to have as its object the Anglo-Saxon domination of the world. Into this world came Mr. Kipling, an able man, believing in these ideas, possessed of practical knowledge from which to argue in their favour, and armed with a style which made it almost impossible not to read him. Hence came his leap into a position in English political thought and feeling which, it is safe to say, no other English imaginative writer (even Milton not excepted) has ever occupied. Hence, too, came the difficulty, which still exists, of looking at him dispassionately as an imaginative writer. We do not often mix together our enjoyment of literature and our partisan interest in politics, but when we do it, we do it thoroughly.

So it comes about that we find even critics who maintain that Mr. Kipling does not write well. But he, that preacher of the gospel of efficiency, lives, in this, up to his own principles. He can write : by which I mean that he obviously never wastes even the merest shaving of his opportunities or of his great natural talents. He appeared in England, comet-like and amazing. His range of themes was exceedingly broad. He wrote about English soldiers in barracks in India, about Simla grass-widows talking among themselves in their own rooms, about the fighting and mating of seals on the beach of Novastoshnah, about Scottish engineers in the engine-rooms of tramp-steamers, and about horses in New England pastures. It was a marvellous display ; and still the wonder grew that one very short lifetime could have included all that he seemed to know.

Perhaps it is no business of the critic to inquire how an author knows what he seems to know : if he convincingly seems to know it, that should be enough. But there are distracting clues to the solution of this problem. In *The Finest Story in the World* Mr. Kipling writes thus :—

" ' One minute, Charlie. When the sea topped the bulwarks what did it look like ? ' I had my reasons for asking. A man of my acquaintance had once gone down with a leaking ship in a still sea, and had seen the water-level pause for an instant ere it fell on the deck.

" ' It looked just like a banjo-string drawn tight, and it seemed to stay there for years," said Charlie.

" Exactly ! The other man had said : ' It looked like a silver wire laid down along the bulwarks, and I thought it was never going to break.' He had paid everything except the bare life for this little valueless piece of knowledge, and I had travelled ten thousand weary miles to meet him and take his knowledge at second-hand. But

Charlie, the bank-clerk on twenty-five shillings a week, who had never been out of sight of a made road, knew it all. It was no consolation to me to know that once in his lives he had been forced to die for his gains. I also must have died scores of times, but behind me, because I could have used my knowledge, the doors were shut."

In this passage, because Mr. Kipling, as I have said, never wastes even the thinnest shaving of his material and always packs everything tight, lie many phrases that betray his secret. He travels " ten thousand weary miles " to get a " little valueless piece of knowledge at second-hand," which, he asserts (this is a trope) he has not been given at first-hand because he could have used his knowledge. We can dismiss Charlie ; but an informant remains. Did he really say : " It looked just like a banjo-string drawn tight, and it seemed to stay there for years " ? Or did Mr. Kipling's visualising genius make that out of something less vivid ?

However the fact may be in the particular instance, Mr. Kipling is a reporter—probably the best reporter who ever lived. The first peculiar gift which made his success was that of being able at once to get a lively and convincing image of a thing, *even at second-hand*. In one of his stories certain subalterns from the East relate their experiences to Eustace Cleever, a celebrated author. At the end—

" He replied with another quotation to the effect that, though singing was a remarkably fine performance, I was to be quite sure that few lips would be moved to song if they could find a sufficiency of kissing. Whereby I understood that Eustace Cleever, decorator and colourman in words, was blaspheming his own Art, and would be sorry for this in the morning."

The quotation is from James Thomson (the later one), an old favourite. It is a motive which occurs more than once in Mr. Kipling's middle period. Earlier he was merely omniscient. In the middle period he is uncomfortably aware of the real sources of his omniscience. Later he grows resigned, mellow, and even a little contentedly humble.

At the beginning it is truly and irritatingly the reporter's omniscience. There is something revealing in the tendency of *Plain Tales from the Hills* to begin with authoritative and far-reaching generalisations :—

"There are more ways of running a horse to suit your book than pulling his head off in the straight. Some men forget this. Understand clearly that all racing is rotten—as everything connected with losing money must be. In India, in addition to its inherent rottenness, it has the merit of being two-thirds sham, looking pretty on paper only. Every one knows every one else far too well for business purposes. How on earth can you rack and harry and post a man for his losings when you are fond of his wife and live in the same Station with him? He says, 'On the Monday following'; 'I can't settle yet.' You say, 'All right, old man,' and think yourself lucky if you pull off nine hundred out of a two-thousand-rupee debt. Any way you look at it, Indian racing is immoral, and expensively immoral ; which is much worse. If a man wants your money he ought to ask for it, or send round a subscription list, instead of juggling about the country with an Australian larrikin ; a 'brumby,' with as much breed as the boy ; a brace of *chumars* in gold-laced caps ; three or four *ekka*-ponies with hogged manes, and a switch-tailed demirep of a mare called Arab because she has a kink in her flag. Racing leads to the *shroff* quicker than anything else. But if you have no conscience and no sentiments, and good hands, and some knowledge of pace, and ten years' experience of horses, and several thousand rupees a month, I believe that you can occasionally contrive to pay your shoeing-bills."

This comes out of the mouth of a man in the very early twenties ; and perhaps, if it were not so well expressed, it would be dismissible as such and therefore less irritating. But it is in fact the gay omniscience of every young man, delivered with a skill in the use of words which makes it impossible to ignore. It is the reporter's gift ; and early life is the time for the reporter to exercise it. He is still young, and his omniscience comes at second-hand ; and just therefore it must be " put over " with every ounce of weight he has at his command. Mr. Kipling's appetite for " putting things over " increased with eating. He was in a position where he must do it if he could. The necessity brought the gift to light ; and the more he found that he could do it, the more diligently he sharpened the one knife that never failed him. He became a marvellous observer. One sees him again and again in his own stories the silent observer, standing carefully back so that he may not frighten the fish.

Nevertheless, this early work, with whatever cunning it may be done, is crude and raw in content. The author's main intention is to score his effect and to do that he hits wherever an opening offers, careless of the direction. Let us take, from *Soldiers Three*, an example at random :—

" ' Fwhat d' you take me for ? ' she sez.

" ' A woman,' sez I ; ' the prettiest in barricks.'

" ' A *wife*,' sez she ; ' the straightest in cantonmints ! '

" Wid that I dropped my arm, fell back tu paces, an' saluted, for I saw that she mint fwhat she said."

" ' Then you know something that some men would give a good deal to be certain of. How could you tell ? ' I demanded in the interests of Science.

" ' Watch the hand,' said Mulvaney ; ' av she shuts her hand tight, thumb down over the knuckle, take up your hat an' go. You'll only make a fool av yoursilf av you shtay. But av the hand lies opin on the lap, or av you see her thryin' to shut ut, an' she can't—go on ! She's not past reasonin' wid.' "

It is all there, the second-hand omniscience, the veneer of realism and the crude sentiment, as immediate and powerful in its attack as wood-alcohol—the whole expressed with admirable economy of words. This is about the love-affairs of N.C.O.'s and other ranks. In the same volume, in that renowned piece, *The Story of the Gadsbys*, Mr. Kipling attacks the love affairs of commissioned officers. It is a renowned piece, and it contains a renowned vulgarity :—

" Miss D. (*abstractedly*) *:* Does he wax that moustache ?

" Miss T. (*busy with powder-puff*) *:* Yes, I think so. Why ?

" Miss D. (*bending over the bodice and sewing furiously*) *:* Oh, nothing—only——

" MISS T. (*sternly*) *:* Only what ? Out with it, Emma.

" MISS D. : Well, May Olger—she's engaged to Mr. Charteris, you know—said—— Promise you won't repeat this ?

" MISS T. : Yes, I promise. What did she say ?

" MISS D. : That—that being kissed (*with a rush*) by a man who *didn't* wax his moustache was —like eating an egg without salt.

" MISS T. (*at her full height*, *with crushing scorn*) : May Olger is a horrid nasty *thing*, and you can tell her I said so. I'm glad she doesn't belong to my set."

But this effect is undoubtedly contrived to demonstrate the theme that a thoroughly trivial young woman, with thoroughly trivial friends, can bring on Captain Gadsby and herself the sufficiently serious experiences—marriage, devotion, fear of separation, a child, the end of his career—that she does bring. One only wishes that Mr. Kipling's determination to drive his point home had not produced, as a sort of by-product, an independent and rather disagreeable effect. In the succeeding scenes all these results are shown with successful ruthlessness. Minnie almost dies after her still-born first child ; and Captain Gadsby and his friend almost weep when the shadow lifts :—

" CAPT. G. (*his head on neck of M.'s charger*) : Jack ! I bub-bub-believe I'm going to make a bub-bub-bloody exhibition of byself.

" CAPT. M. (*sniffing openly and feeling in his left cuff*) : I'b-b—I'b doing it already. Old bad, what *cad* I say ? I'b as pleased as—God *dab* you, Gaddy ! You're one big idiot and I'b adother ! "

It is by no means hard to cry with Captain Gadsby and Captain Mafflin : in fact, it would prove either extreme cynicism or extreme ignorance of life if one had no temptation to do so. But when the fit is over one resents the unfair trick that has been played on one. It seems to the reader a pity that the young giant should be so ignorant of his own strength as to imagine that he is under any necessity of hitting below the belt.

This unfair excess in the use of power may prove inexperience and a certain and peculiar lack of self-confidence. It ought not to suggest lack of competence. Mr. Kipling's ability to produce a definite effect in his own medium should never have been in doubt. He has an instinct for words and for the rhythms in which words may be used, and often shows it in a startling way. His poem called *Boots* (*Infantry Columns*) has an almost maddening effect on the mind :—

" Try—try—try—try—to think o' something different—
O—my—God—keep—me from goin' lunatic !
(Boots—boots—boots—boots—movin' up an' down again !)
There's no discharge in the war !

Count—count—count—count—the bullets in the bandoliers.
If—your—eyes—drop—they will get atop o' you—
(Boots—boots—boots—boots—movin' up an' down again !)
There's no discharge in the war ! "

It gives the movement of tired men on the march with a truth beyond admiration ; and it brings itself home even to readers who have never been in that state. Such renderings of physical things are surprising and effective and difficult, just because they are rarely attempted. But in nearly all his short stories Mr. Kipling approaches the rendering of subtler things with equal confidence in the power of words rightly used. His prose, even at the beginning, is a subtle and accomplished instrument. It is never what is meant by the opprobrious term "mechanical": it is never dull and monotonous. But it often has the movement of one of those complicated machines which he himself, with many technical terms, loves to describe. The wheels revolve, levers appear and disappear, curious well-adapted appliances come into sight for a moment and are gone again. There is a rhythm and a repetition but it is manifold and various in its details; and the mind is not made weary by seeing the same things too soon again.

This is in the short stories. There was a sensation when Mr. Kipling attempted a novel; and the sensation of the failure is still looked back to, in spite of the fact that in a further attempt, in *Kim*, he has more or less succeeded. But *The Light that Failed* showed that he faltered on a long flight, though he had been so secure on short flights. And, though other points might be criticised, the principal weakness of the book lies in the fact that Mr. Kipling does not seem able to maintain the consistency of his characters over so long a span. The two children, Dick and Maisie, are well drawn; the two adults they eventually become are well drawn; but between the two pairs there is no recognisable connection. At the beginning Mrs. Jennett objects to Maisie's goat:—

"'Then,' said the atom, choosing her words very deliberately, 'I shall write to my lawyer peoples and tell them that you are a very bad woman. Amomma is mine, mine, mine!' Mrs. Jennet made a movement to the hall, where certain umbrellas and canes stood in a rack. The atom understood as clearly as Dick what this meant. 'I have been beaten before,' she said, still in the same passionless voice; 'I have been beaten worse than you can ever beat me. If you beat me I shall write to my lawyer peoples and tell them you do not give me enough to eat. I am not afraid of you.'"

How could this decisive and strong-charactered child grow into the characterless girl who afterwards fails Dick merely for want of strength and clings on feebly to a vocation in which she has no hope of real success but from which she still hopes to obtain a few laudatory press-cuttings? Her inability to rise to the occasion and make a real use of herself in something real provides the little flame of observed life which illuminates the second half of the book. This is an excellent study of character and motive (Dick's own attitude is a trifle stagey) so far as it goes. But it does not go very far. The rest of the story, with the girl who ruins Dick's picture while he is asleep, sticks out her tongue at him and whispers "Bilked!" as she escapes, is merely clever vamping. It is well done: it fills up the space round the small fragment of important truth which Mr. Kipling has to tell. but it is cheaply crude in conception, at best a skilful playing on the nerves of the reader; and again one regrets that so much skill should be wasted on a thing so little worth doing.

In *Kim* this inability to cover a long span is not so noticeable. *Kim* has not the organic construction and development of a story. The tale of Kim's birth and its discovery, of his upbringing and of his first great adventure in men's work, is not very interesting and does not so much hold the attention that one fails to observe how often, as a tale, it flags. The importance of the book lies in its long, leisurely portrayal of British India, in its assemblage of vividly sketched persons, among whom the old Lama, thoroughly understood and beautifully represented, is the best. The Lama is indeed perhaps the best of all Mr. Kipling's characters. He is shown at more length, and with more result for the length than any other.

But undoubtedly Mr. Kipling's gift is rather for the sudden light on character which can be thrown in a short story than for any continuous or exhaustive exposition. Certain characters occur again and again in his tales—Stalky and his companions, Mulvaney, Learoyd, and Ortheris. But there is never any attempt at development. The effect of character is built up just enough to make each episode credible and solid, and no more. It is worth remarking that the adventures of Stalky, Beetle, and M'Turk begin at a point when, as schoolboys at least, they are beyond change. And indeed they do not change from the moment at which they trespass on Colonel Dabney's estate to that in which they bribe Mary Yeo to kiss Tulke. Stalky appears once again as a subaltern, when he might still be a schoolboy, and once again as a battalion-commander—when he might be anybody. It is when Mr. Kipling attempts something out of his range that he betrays his worst weakness. This worst weakness is the tendency to use his gifts of personality, persuasion, and vividness, his reporter's gifts, to "put over" something not worthy of the resources lavished on it. When he thus exerts himself he secures what may be called a triumph of brute strength over the good taste which is too delicate properly to defend itself. One's first admiration of Mr. Kipling too often leaves behind it a feeling of having been overcome by unfair force ; but if he uses brute strength, he also admires it and judges only on immediate results.

In the short stories, however, this temptation to him can be, by the nature of the thing, absent throughout an entire piece. And as a writer of short stories he does undoubtedly come first in the English language. Mr. Wells, to take one example, who was obviously much influenced by him, deserves to be mentioned in the same category. But Mr. Wells has attempted other things (and succeeded with them), and has not given the whole of his time or the best of his wits to this particular form, in which he has not Mr. Kipling's range or his variety. There are others, but space is too short to mention them here. The canon of Mr. Kipling includes some fourteen volumes ; and the stories are of all sorts, gay and grave, exotic and domestic. The classification of them would make an admirable theme for a *Doktorfrage* ; but, having said something already on the diversity of their subjects, I must leave that alone.

The point to be observed is that here can be seen the curve of Mr. Kipling's development from the early arrogance of—

"He heard the sound that a man never forgets all his life—the '*ah-yah*' of an angry crowd.

(When that sound drops about three tones, and changes to a thick, droning *ut*, the man who hears it had better go away if he is alone.)"

through the somewhat uneasy maturity of *The Finest Story in the World* to the mellow and golden autumn of *Friendly Brook*. It is as though Indian suns (but surely he was not very long in India) had saturated him with raw light, which it has needed decades of more temperate weather to soak out of him again. His gift of understanding, of seizing the heart of a situation, was never in doubt. In *The Flag of Their Country* he shows to the full his understanding of the reticence of the ordinarily brought-up public-school boy in the face of public emotion :—

"Now, the reserve of a boy is tenfold deeper than the reserve of a maid, she being made for one end only by blind Nature, but man for several. With a large and healthy hand he tore down the veils, and trampled them under the well-intentioned feet of eloquence. In a raucous voice he cried aloud little matters, like the hope of Honour and the dream of Glory, that boys do not discuss even with their most intimate equals—cheerfully assuming that, till he spoke, they had never considered these possibilities. He pointed them to shining goals, with fingers which smudged out all radiance on all horizons. He profaned the most secret places of their souls with outcries and gesticulations. He bade them consider the deeds of their ancestors in such a fashion that they were flushed to their tingling ears. Some of them—the rending voice cut a frozen stillness—might have had relatives who perished in defence of their country. (They thought, not a few of them, of an old sword in a passage, or above a breakfast-room table, seen and fingered by stealth since they could walk.) He adjured them to emulate those illustrious examples ; and they looked all ways in their extreme discomfort."

It is all true ; but are there not boys who, reading it, have suffered something of the discomfort felt by Stalky and his friends when they were bound down to listen to the eloquence of Mr. Raymond Martin, M.P. ? One marvels that so close a realisation of the diffidence of boyhood can go with so much flamboyance of expression. It is, again, the reporter's gift. Mr. Kipling understands ; but, having understood, he will use any means to drive his point into the reader's head. There was for long about his work something of the violence of the sun of India and something of the raw impatience of new countries.

There are those indeed who consider that Mr. Kipling deservedly made his reputation in the early 'nineties and that since then he has been nothing but a shadow of his younger self. Yet, it may be proper to ask, may not the shadows cast by so violent a light prove to be of more value than its own rays ? For me, at any rate, up to the publication of his last collection of stories, Mr. Kipling's work has grown increasingly satisfying. The dazzling, enchanting skill remains ; but the rawness and violence of the feelings, or the appeal to the reader's feelings, is diminished. The first ponderable sign of the change is marked perhaps by the publication of *Kim* in 1901. It appears in such stories as *An Habitation Enforced* and in the gracious details of *Puck of Pook's Hill* and *Rewards and Fairies.* In *Friendly Brook* the exquisite power of description is as strong as ever it was :—

" The valley was so choked with fog that one could hardly see a cow's length across a field. Every blade, twig, bracken-frond and hoof-print carried water, and the air was filled with the noise of rushing ditches and field-drains, all delivering to the brook below. A week's November rain on water-logged land had gorged her to full flood, and she proclaimed it aloud.

" Two men in sackcloth aprons were considering an untrimmed hedge that ran down the hillside and disappeared into mist beside those roarings. They stood back and took stock of the neglected growth, tapped an elbow of hedge-oak here, a mossed beech-stub there, swayed a stooled ash back and forth, and looked at each other."

The picture is complete and perfect. The story which follows it is simply that of the attachment of a Sussex peasant to the abandoned child whom he has received from " one o' those Lunnon Childern Societies." He loves her, and when her unworthy father claims her, he pays hush-money, until Friendly Brook conveniently drowns the man. Therefore Jim Wickenden says, " The Brook's been good friends to me, and if she be minded to take a snatch at my hay, *I* ain't settin' out to withstand her." The thread is simple ; but Mr. Kipling makes it carry a good deal. This, if one had to select an example of his work for an anthology of short stories, might well be one's first choice. There are four or five which follow it closely ; and all have been written in the second half of his career.

I may have seemed to write sneeringly or slightingly of much of Mr. Kipling's earlier work. If one considers his writings as a whole one is haunted by a sense of huge talents taking too often a path of least resistance which an equally admirable ingenuity much too easily discovers. Thus haunted, it is only too easy to fail to give any impression of his range and versatility, to forget to mention with the rest such things as the solid, satisfying horseplay of *My Sunday at Home*, *Brugglesmith*, and *The Village that Voted the Earth was Flat*. But even where one sneers, even where one sees qualities improvable and improved by time, one quality is always obvious and must not be denied. There is an immense vitality in all this work. It has, for good or evil, set a fashion of surprising endurance and nothing without vitality could ever have set a fashion which endured so long. Mr. Kipling may have learnt—he certainly did from Poe and Stevenson, he may have done from Maupassant, but his is the spirit which beyond dispute can be traced in almost every page of the popular magazines both in England and in America.

When we come to look at his verse the same thing must be said. Most of it is rhetoric ; but little of it is ineffective rhetoric. There is much to be said against such writing as this :—

" Tom Hall stood up by the quarter-rail. 'Your words in your teeth,' said he.
'There's never a law of God or man runs north of Fifty-Three.
So go in grace with Him to face, and an ill-spent life behind,
And I'll be good to your widows, Rube, as many as I shall find.'

A Stralsund man shot blind and large, and a warlock Finn was he,
And he hit Tom Hall with a bursting ball a hand's-breadth over the knee.
Tom Hall caught hold by the topping-lift, and sat him down with an oath.
'You'll wait a little, Rube,' he said. 'The devil has called for both.
The Devil is driving both this tide and the killing-grounds are close,
And we'll go up to the wrath of God as the holluschickie goes.
O men, put back your guns again and lay your rifles by,
We've fought our fight, and the best are down. Let up and let us die!
Quit firing, by the bow there—quit! Call off the *Baltic's* crew!
You're sure of Hell as me or Rube—but wait till we get through.' "

One is inclined to begin by saying that the worst against this style is that it has raised up to itself so great a crop of quite intolerable imitations. But this very fact is, as a phenomenon, worthy of notice and even of admiration. Uncountable poets have been pricked to imitation and a large public applauds them. This is due no doubt to the fact that two or three generations in large, well-policed towns have engendered in our race a platonic and disinterested love of violence; but it must be recorded that Mr. Kipling was the first man to put this dumb feeling into words. The style is bold and coarse. It derives from old ballads, but its boldness springs, not as there from naïve instinct, but perceptibly from civilised cunning. Its flavour is therefore different. Its swinging gait, deliberately adopted, is too mechanical to merge into the milder intimacies and humanities of the ballad.

But there are moments when Mr. Kipling, clearly with the same model in mind, gets nearer to the original. His besetting weakness is the desire to make an effect by the quickest and surest means : this style is a short cut to an effect. But occasionally—and often enough to make the sum of all the occasions impressive—his feeling about his subject quite overcomes this weakness. Real feeling comes through in even *Gentlemen Rankers* (which is an example of an intermediary type between the ballad and the music-hall song) and more poignantly in *Ford o' Kabul River.* When we consider the dialect poems, it must be admitted that Mr. Kipling has once or twice raised the Cockney speech to the dignity of a poetic tongue:—

"The Injian Ocean sets an' smiles
So sof', so bright, so bloomin' blue ;
There aren't a wave for miles an' miles
Excep' the jiggle from the screw.
The ship is swep', the day is done,
The bugle's gone for smoke and play ;
An' black ag'in the settin' sun
The Lascar sings: 'Hum deckty hai !'

For to admire an' for to see
For to be'old this world so wide—
It never done no good to me,
But I can't drop it if I tried !

. . . .

Oh, I 'ave come upon the books,
An' frequent broke a barrick rule,

An' stood beside an' watched myself
    Be'avin' like a bloomin' fool.
I paid my price for findin' out,
    Nor never grutched the price I paid,
But sat in Clink without my boots,
    Admirin' 'ow the world was made."

It is philosophical and beautiful, and, as an indispensable preliminary to these, it is sincere. The dialect might have been used patronisingly, merely with a view to "quaintness." But here the feeling of the poem transcends the accidents of the language and merely fixes them as part of its final success.

Thus it is throughout the whole of Mr. Kipling's work. He has always been described as a precocious writer; and it is very generally assumed that his early brilliance necessarily entailed exhausted and disappointing later years. It would probably be nearer the truth to say that those gifts which in him were the earliest to display themselves needed time and hard work before they could be brought into their proper place. This prophet of co-ordination has found it no easy matter to co-ordinate his own talents. Now, and for some years past, he writes very little. But in most of what he writes now those early brilliant faults have been subdued and have become useful subsidiary virtues.

Mr. Joseph Conrad

When Mr. Conrad, nearly thirty years ago, began his career as a novelist, English readers and critics had just begun to get used to a new sort of literature. I mean the literature which found material in the stranger and obscurer parts of the world, not for romance and fantasy but for a realism which had nevertheless colours as high and garish, qualities as unexpected, as any romance could be expected to have. We became then suddenly aware that real white men, originally, it was to be presumed, exactly like ourselves, were living real daily lives in countries quite unlike our own. In these countries adventure and mystery were more common than with us and they gave an opportunity for the introduction of a new flavour into literature, the flavour of realistic adventure and realistic mystery. A sort of imperialistic fiction became all the rage ; and there was as it were a certain informative air about its details, which made them look as self-conscious as the products of foreign countries set out under the glass cases of an exhibition.

And so Mr. Conrad, publishing his first novel, had to protest that, though he had written about a tragic Dutchman marooned up a river in Borneo among Arabs and Malays, his intention was not that of the writers with whom he was so obviously to be confounded. The picture of life, he says in the preface to that first book,

" there as here, is drawn with the same elaboration of detail, coloured with the same tints. Only in the cruel serenity of the sky, under the merciless brilliance of the sun, the dazzled eye misses the delicate detail, sees only the strong outlines, while the colours, in the steady light, seem crude and without shadow. Nevertheless it is the same picture."

And he adds that what is everywhere the same and everywhere interesting is the heart of man.

The claim is in the main a just one. Wherever Mr. Conrad sets his scene, whether on the high seas or among the shallows of the Eastern archipelagos, he never allows his background to degenerate into mere " local colour " or gives it too much attention merely because it is strange. His concern is that of all great novelists, to make a picture of life ; his subject is theirs, the heart of man. And because he is sincere in his purpose, he deals very easily with a particular world the strangeness of which, however brilliantly presented, would overwhelm the genius of any writer less single-minded, less intensely concentrated on a single aim.

He would say, perhaps, that he has written mostly of ships and much of the East because that is the life he happens to know. It is an accident. For him, as I shall try presently to show, it has been a very fortunate accident. But as accidental to the real content of his work he himself evidently regards it. It has never been his first aim to give to the shore-folk of the West a picture of seafaring in the East. His first aim has been a picture of life ; and a novelist must have some materials with which to embody his vision of life. Mr. Conrad took the materials which came readiest to him.

But to write on Mr. Conrad without first discussing two remarkable, if very well-known, facts of his career would be almost to insult the conventions of modern criticism. He was for many years an officer in the English mercantile marine, and began to be a novelist only comparatively late in life, after he had retired from that profession. Further, though he has been an English sea captain, and is now an English novelist, he is not an Englishman by birth, but of pure Polish blood.

It is not easy to be sure which of these facts is generally regarded as the more extraordinary, though of Mr. Conrad's own opinion there can be no doubt. He was once at some pains to rebut a prevalent opinion that, at the outset of his literary career, he exercised a deliberate choice between English and French as the language for his books. This, if it had been true, would have been extraordinary indeed ; but it was not true. " My recollection," he tells us, " of what I meant to say is : that *had I been under the necessity* of making a choice between the two, and though I knew French fairly well, and was familiar with it from infancy, I would have been afraid to attempt expression in a language so perfectly ' crystallised.' " And he goes on to say that : " the truth of the matter is that my faculty to write in English is as natural as any other aptitude with which I might have been born. I have a strange and overpowering feeling that it had always been an inherent part of myself. English was for me neither a matter of choice nor adoption."

There is a suggestion here that Mr. Conrad would hardly have thought about the matter at all if his attention had not been drawn to it by what evidently seems to him an astonishing misconception. He realises with his mind that it *is* strange that he should write in English, but in his heart he cannot feel it to be strange at all. (It may be noted that, so far as his readers are informed, the question whether he might not have written in Polish never once occurred to him) On the other hand he refers more than once to those many years of his life when nothing could have seemed madder than a prophecy that later on he would become an author in any language. Literary ambition, he said, had never entered into the world of his imagination ; and several times he unconsciously betrays an almost naïve surprise that he should have written not merely his first, but equally his tenth or his twentieth book.

And yet this is really hardly at all surprising. It is not difficult, it seems, to write a book : any one can do it ; very many persons do : one never knows who will do it next. But the matter of the language is more extraordinary. For Mr. Conrad has not only brought it off pretty well, and succeeded in making himself intelligible. He has, and has had from his first page, a definite style of his own, which, strongly marked as it is, cannot be said to be in any way foreign to the genius of our language, a style fitted for expressing the subtlest shades of meaning, and the most obscure and complex emotions. It is a poetic and evocative style, which does not and could not build itself up from the naked literal senses of words. It uses those vague associations of words, those overtones which even natives cannot explain and which, one would think, only natives could successfully employ. Moreover, I do not believe that Mr. Conrad has ever at any stage had to have his English " vetted " as Oscar Wilde had to have the surely much simpler and easier French of *Salome*.

It is true, I think, that careful search would reveal traces of a foreign hand. There is a little uncertainty in Mr. Conrad's handling of "shall" and "will." He has occasional difficulties with his tenses, and one finds certain forms ("faculty to write," in the quotation above, is an example) which are not precisely incorrect, but which are not customary in English. But these are only details of the surface, and affect the reader no more than such trifling carelessnesses as may be found in any author: such mistakes as any reader can correct for himself (*e.g.*, infinitives inadvertently split) have no more to do with style than have printer's errors. The essential fact is that Mr. Conrad has possessed himself of the English language, and uses it to express things which would be hard enough for a man to express in his own native tongue. He has done more: he has made a definite impression on the English style of his time, some would even say too deep an impression, for his is a fatally attractive manner to copy. Be that as it may, many English writers have taken from the Pole lessons in the writing of English. And since his books contain many pages which seize the attention not merely by their feeling and atmosphere and colour, but also by the rhythm of the sentences and the sonorous beauty of the language, it is absurd to speak of them, as some one has done, as "translations of French novels which will never be written."

There is in this, no doubt, much that we cannot explain: it might be accounted for by some freak in the convolutions of the brain. But it is hard not to suppose that the very difficulty of the task has had something to do with Mr. Conrad's success in it. For "the fascination of what's difficult" has been a very potent factor throughout the whole of his career. It has not dried the blood out of his veins, but it has stimulated him often to the extraction of more than one would have thought possible from a given subject, and sometimes to feats of marvellous sleight-of-hand in narration. This last, on at least one occasion, provoked in himself a feeling of almost comical bewilderment. He says of *The Return* :—

" Looking through that story lately I had the material impression of sitting under a large and expensive umbrella, in the loud drumming of a furious rain-shower. It was very distracting. In the general uproar one could hear every individual drop strike on the stout and distended silk. Mentally, the reading rendered me dumb for the remainder of the day, not exactly with astonishment, but with a sort of dismal wonder. I don't want to talk disrespectfully of any pages of mine. Psychologically there were, no doubt, good reasons for my attempt ; and it was worth while if only to see of what excesses I was capable in that sort of virtuosity. In this connection I should like to confess my surprise on finding that, notwithstanding all its apparatus of analysis, the story consists for the most part of physical impressions, impressions of sound and sight, railway station, streets, a trotting horse, reflections in mirrors, and so on, rendered as if for their sake, and combined with a sublimated description of a desirable middle-class town-residence, which somehow manages to produce a sinister effect."

This is an admirable description and criticism of a piece of work which is, to be sure, rather an empty thing. In *The Return* a self-complacent husband comes home to find, without the least warning, that his wife, tired of his self-complacency and nullity, has run away with another man. And she, finding herself also bound by the respectability which had so wearied her in her husband, cannot bring herself to go through with the elopement, and returns after an absence of only an hour or so. They make a dazed effort for a little while to preserve respectable appearances, but the bottom has fallen out of the husband's world, and the same night he leaves his home for ever. No doubt there are possibilities of life and vision in this story : there are, indeed, in all stories. But Mr. Conrad has left them alone. The two persons awake neither his love nor his anger, nor yet, as persons, the reader's interest. The interest of the piece of work is confined purely to a series of dazzling and difficult feats of impressionism, such as the description of the servant going up to bed :—

" He saw her come up gradually, as if ascending from a well. At every step the feeble flame of the candle swayed before her tired young face, and the darkness of the hall seemed to cling to her black skirt, followed her, rising like a silent flood, as though the great night of the world had broken through the discreet reserve of walls, of closed doors, of curtained windows. It rose over the steps, it leaped up the walls like an angry wave, it flowed over the blue skies, over the yellow sands, over the sunshine of landscapes, and over the pretty pathos of ragged innocence and meek starvation. It swallowed up the delicious idyll and the mutilated immortality of famous bas-reliefs. It flowed from outside—it rose higher, in a destructive silence. And above it, the woman of marble, composed and blind on the high pedestal, seemed to ward off the devouring night with a cluster of lights."

It is magnificent and strangely purposeless. It is strikingly too elaborate, for it is only a background for characters whose personalities and emotions have not been made significant to us.

But Mr. Conrad does not as a rule set himself such difficulties of the acrobat as this. He does not defend *The Return* : he supposes, faintly, that he must have had some reason for writing it. But on other occasions when he has been reproved for excessive ingenuity and elaboration he is ready to defend himself. He says in the preface to *Chance* :—

"Captain Anthony's determination led him a long and roundabout course and that is why this book is a long book. A critic has remarked that if I had selected another method of composition and taken a little more trouble the tale would have been told in about two hundred pages. I confess I do not perceive exactly the bearings of such criticism or even the use of such a remark. No doubt that by selecting a certain method and taking great pains the whole story might have been written out on a cigarette paper."

And generally he is ready to show, where we cannot see for ourselves, that his unexpected technical tricks and ingenuities have been devised with great care, not for their own sake but in order to get the story told and to express what the story meant for the author.

These self-critical prefaces, from which I have twice made quotations, are among the most interesting confessions ever made by a creative artist in literature. Mr. Conrad is, in the good sense, a very self-conscious writer : he never does anything without knowing why, and he takes a strong pleasure in the expedients which he has deliberately planned. I must not delay too long over this side of my subject but a few more comments on it may be permitted before I go further.

It is worth while, for example, to remark on the peculiar manner in which the story of *The Nigger of the Narcissus* gets itself told. This is simply the tale of a ship's company and how, in spite of internal difficulties and quarrels, it fights its way through great dangers and accomplishes its ordinary duty. It might be called the first study in "Unanimism," a form of literature in which the group is more important than the individual, but it is not so rigidly ingenious as the works of the French writers who once adopted that label. There is a personal narrator who contrives, however, quite extraordinarily, to be no more than one of the group. He occasionally makes it clear that he witnessed and took part in the events he describes by saying that "groaning, we dug our fingers in, and very much hurt, shook our hands, scattering nails, and drops of blood" or by remarking on "the conceited folly of us all." Never was there in fiction so complete a suppression of the personality of the eye-witness and never was it more necessary. The word "I" does not occur, I think, until the very end of the book, when it suddenly becomes effective, as, after the crew has been paid off, the narrator stands and watches his late companions, those who have suffered and struggled with him, scattering into the surroundings of the docks :—

"I never saw them again. The sea took some, the steamers took others, the graveyards of the earth will account for the rest. Singleton has no doubt taken with him the long record of his faithful work into the peaceful depths of an hospitable sea. And Donkin, who never did a decent day's work in his life, no doubt earns his living by discoursing with filthy eloquence upon the right of labour to live. So be it. Let the earth and the sea have each its own."

One must comment too on the ease and lucidity with which Mr. Conrad handles the complicated nest of Chinese boxes which makes up the story of *Chance*. Some person unspecified relates what Marlowe told him about what Fyne told him about the childhood of Flora de Barral ; and one is never confused, never forgets the precise source of the information which the page is at any given moment communicating. So with all the tales in which Marlowe acts as informant, collecting the facts and piecing them together. It is a complicated and exceedingly difficult method, but one which Mr. Conrad has adopted so as to be able, so to speak, to look all round his story, to give it the distances and gradations of life, and one which he uses with as much triumphant confidence as he uses the English language.

But what is it that needs all this array of difficulties and intricate technical expedients ? Not just the telling of stories surely, for we all know that a plain tale is best plainly told. It is quite simply the presentation of a particular and individual vision of life, and of this too Mr. Conrad is fully conscious. He says :—

" Those who read me know my conviction that the world, the temporal world, rests on a few very simple ideas : so simple that they must be as old as the hills. It rests notably, among others, on the idea of Fidelity."

Indeed almost the whole of Mr. Conrad's work is the confession in a concrete form of his fidelity to this belief. The fact that he has given us a brilliantly varied collection of tales and persons does not alter the fact that he has been in effect saying the same thing over and over again.

Attempts have been made to explain his books as being not novels but modern epics which happen to be written in prose. I am not sure that there is much to be gained by this sort of juggling with terminology ; but it is true that his stories are sharply differentiated from the novel as it has been developed during the last hundred years. The modern novel of psychology and character is essentially an art of complication. It has gradually come to have as its chief aim the representation of the development of character, the faithful painting of the changes of personality. This it sets above the telling of a story, and, in an even greater degree, above the presentment of general ideas. Hence Mr. Lubbock's recent rather despairing search for form in the novel, his complaint that it is difficult to hold a novel as a whole in one's mind.

Mr. Conrad's aim is different and simpler. In one sense it is true that the story of any one of his books might be written out on a cigarette paper, or one might say that it would cause one no surprise to find prefixed to them such " arguments " as are used to define the scope of epics. Or one might compare the whole series of them to a modern *Faërie Queene* with each book illustrating a moral quality. And it is just to say that, for example, in *The Rescue*, Lingard's faithfulness to those who trust in him is as simple and as governing a theme as the wrath of Achilles.

But let us take one instance on which the author has said an illuminating thing. Referring to the obvious connection between *The Arrow of Gold* and a certain story told in *The Mirror of the Sea*, he says :—

" For the purposes of a book like *The Mirror of the Sea* all I could make use of was the personal history of the little *Tremolino*. The present work is not in any sense an attempt to develop a subject lightly touched upon in former years and in connection with quite another kind of love. What the story of the *Tremolino* in its anecdotic character has in common with the story of *The Arrow of Gold* is the quality of initiation (through an ordeal which required some resolution to face) into the life of passion. In the few pages at the end of *The Mirror of the Sea* and in the whole of the volume of *The Arrow of Gold*, *that* and no other is the subject offered to the public. The pages and the book form together a complete record ; and the only assurance I can give my readers is, that as it stands here with all its imperfections it is given to them complete."

In the one story the boat, the *Tremolino*, in the other the woman, Dona Rita ; and both lead the writer to the *idea* of " initiation into the life of passion." The seeker after autobiographical details will not find this explanation very enlightening. Dona Rita appears also in *The Mirror of the Sea* and there she has " the volatile little soul of a sparrow dressed in fine Parisian feathers, which had the trick of coming off disconcertingly at unexpected moments," while in *The Arrow of Gold* she is the most enchanting and tragic of Mr. Conrad's heroines, the most living and lovable woman in all his books. But the point here to be made is that any incident which comes within his experience (he says, probably with truth, that his inventive faculty was never very strong) awakes in his mind a strong consciousness of the general idea it exemplifies.

This essential and governing characteristic makes its influence felt throughout Mr. Conrad's work. It makes him the novelist of situation rather than of character. His persons develop little, if at all, before our eyes. Sometimes in a retrospective note he tells us how they came to be what he shows them to be. He goes back and shows us how Dr. Monygham had his peculiar sardonic self-contempt stamped on him, how Charles Gould acquired his devotion to the silver mines. In the same book, Nostromo's character changes, to be sure, but it is a single catastrophic change and it is itself the subject of the story.

On the whole it is fair to say that Mr. Conrad devotes no more time to character-drawing than is necessary to secure the liveliness and truth of his situation. Sometimes this betrays him into a weakness, as with the horrific Mr. Jones in *Victory*. Mr. Conrad saw the prototype of this personage once for a moment in an hotel in the West Indies and heard one remark made of him. This memory seemed (or so I conjecture) to fit very well just the sort of wickedness required to create the situation aimed at, to invade the peaceful island of Samburan and to bring about the destruction of Axel Heyst and Lena. But I doubt if many readers have felt convinced by this wickedness : one begins to feel the difficulty of conviction when the author is forced to put into the mouth of Ricardo so many vehement declarations of Mr. Jones's terrible nature.

But such failures are rare. For the most part Mr. Conrad draws in his characters with a few strong lines, charged with force and life ; and it is not often that we feel any necessity of stopping and asking ourselves what we know of these persons. What after all do we know of Lord Jim ? Or of Mr. Verloc in *The Secret Agent* ? Or of Captain McWhirr in *Typhoon* ? Not as much certainly as we do of the major characters of most of the great novelists, not as much as we do of Mr. Micawber or Becky Sharp or Elizabeth Bennett.

Captain McWhirr is almost a type. Mr. Conrad heard an anecdote about a storm and it seized his imagination. But before he could see any eternal significance in the picture of the storm, Captain McWhirr was necessary and Captain McWhirr was accordingly invented. Neither exclusively a storm-piece nor exclusively symbolic, says the author : " both the typhoon and Captain McWhirr presented themselves to me as the necessities of the deep conviction with which I approached the subject of the story." And this subject ? Mr. Conrad declines to explain in a formula that to which he has devoted so many pages. But we can say perhaps that *Typhoon* expresses his passionate appreciation of the spectacle of an ordinary human soul pursuing its way amid terrific turmoils of nature. We know no more of Captain McWhirr than is needed to enable us to make this appreciation our own.

In the same preface Mr. Conrad remarks, it is true, that in most of his writings he insists not on the events but on their effect upon the persons in the tale. There seems to me to be in this a slight misplacing of emphasis. The persons are not indeed, as in many stories of adventure, mere lay figures invented for the sake of the events. But persons and events together make the material which Mr. Conrad uses for the embodiment of his vision of life ; and thus to assign the pre-eminence suggests the manner of those modern novels in which assuredly the events are devised (and not always with much imagination or gusto) for the sake of the persons. I think it is fair to say that one of the qualities which most obviously distinguish Mr. Conrad from his contemporaries in the novel is the *necessity* of the events in his stories.

This clearly connotes the possession of dramatic power ; and the construction of his books is often reminiscent of the economy of a practised dramatist. He is never careless with material ; and when he takes pains to make a fact vivid to us it is because that fact will presently have a direct bearing on the central point of the story. When horrible life and reality are given to the scene in which the governess lets loose her hatred on the wretched child, Flora de Barral, it is because, to take her place in the later situation, Flora must have a strong inward sense that it is natural to hate her, impossible to love her. When guilt for the destruction of the idiot-boy is to be fixed on Mr. Verloc, we have it carefully shown to us, early in the story, that the boy bore on his clothing marks of identification. We are told of this very naturally in a description of Winnie's maternal care of her unfortunate brother ; but, as was intended, we remember the small detail later on.

It is worth noting too how often single scenes

from Mr. Conrad's novels linger vividly in the memory as pictures. There is a scene in *Victory* when the Chinese servant becomes aware of the silent struggle between Ricardo and Lena by the bulges made by the bodies in the curtain which hides them. There is the extraordinary scene in *The Arrow of Gold* when Rita and Monsieur George stand together in silence and in terror listening to the obscene ravings of the lunatic outside the locked doors. From Mr. Conrad's simplification of character and from his insistence on events follows the necessity that whatever scene he attempts should make at any rate a powerful physical impact on the reader. And this necessity is amply met. It is the excuse for *The Return*, that story which so much perplexes the author who wrote it.

I have said that Mr. Conrad has never exploited the unusual character of his experience, but that he has been lucky in it. By this I mean that a genius which would, somehow, anyhow, have struggled to expression was remarkably favoured by fortune during the years in which it was storing up impressions as future material. Mr. Conrad's novels are the expressions of general ideas, of wide and widely applicable appreciations of life. To say that they are of the poetic order might seem either unjustly to deny this rank to the novels of other writers, who must have this quality if their novels are to have any enduring value, or else ridiculously to limit the meaning of the word. But Mr. Conrad has in a striking manner emphasised the poetic, the visionary qualities of the novel. He has written his novels in the world of ideas and visions, the world in which the tragedies of the Greeks and of Shakespeare originated.

Who dare say that without the help of his peculiar experience he might never have done so? But the favour of fortune is perceptible. The expression of general ideas requires some removal from the accidental and confusing details of every-day life as we know it. The Greeks found this removal in myths of the heroic age, Shakespeare in one region or another of romance. Mr. Conrad finds it in the life of the sea and of mysterious Eastern islands, where his persons can develop their ideal proportions, where his events can attain to their ideal significances. The habit of our age, to which all artists are subject, has compelled him to impose on his work a brilliant and seemingly realistic surface. But the idealistic, the truly poetic purpose remains beneath; and this is what is essential in Mr. Conrad.

The peculiarities of his work make his ultimate influence on the English novel very difficult to assess. Mr. Kipling very naturally took our short-story writers into the world east of Suez where there were all manner of new and acute sensations to be exploited. Mr. Conrad, who has never exploited anything, has, if any, an obscurer and subtler influence. But, though it is hardly yet perceptible in the English novel, that influence must sooner or later make itself felt.

His influence on English prose is of course immediate and obvious. He has simply transplanted into English just as many French forms and sentence constructions as the genius of our language will endure; and I do not think that we have suffered by the cross-fertilisation. His achievement in the art of fiction is less easy to see because it is so much larger a thing. When I say that he is supremely the great artist and the great poet among

English novelists, I do not mean to dare the assertion that he is the greatest of English novelists. I do mean that among them all he has most purely the temperament of the literary artist and that therefore he shows most clearly to be seen that spirit of poetic impulse which makes the novel, as it makes any other literary form. The effect of Mr. Conrad's work has been, in the end, to bring the novel back closer to its first source of inspiration, to the impassioned contemplation of ideas. Those who are affected by him need not write of sea-captains or of lagoons in the Indian Ocean. They may write of City clerks or of agricultural labourers; but his influence will certainly show itself in more than superficial imitation.

Mr. John Galsworthy

WHEN Matthew Arnold said that Literature was a criticism of life, he made a statement which has been very freely misunderstood and which has, therefore, been perhaps rather more mischievous than otherwise. But he might have been looking forward to an age of transition, which in his time was almost upon the world, of which indeed he was one of the harbingers, and the effect of which upon literature, has been, in a way, to justify the common misunderstanding of his dictum. He might, that is to say, have foreseen the advent of such authors as Mr. John Galsworthy.

Mr. Galsworthy, whether in the theatre or in the novel, is nothing if not a definite and, in intention at any rate, a practical critic of the institutions of modern life. He is, as we shall see, something more than this ; but he is this in the first place. Almost everywhere throughout his work two types are strongly contrasted. We have on the one hand the upholder of established institutions, who generally belongs to the "Haves," and on the other the rebel or the vagabond, who frequently belongs to the "Have-nots." Mr. Galsworthy appears to see life almost exclusively in these terms : these make up the framework of his world. And in this his work accurately reflects the epoch to which he properly belongs : the epoch when the Fabian Society was an almost unseen but much-felt power, when Mr. Granville Barker's heroes aspired to the sober ideal of useful work in municipal politics, when Mr. Wells's undergraduates sat round the fire and discussed the Problem of Sex.

Many problems have vexed the soul of Mr. Galsworthy. He is troubled by the fact that there is in reality one law for the rich and another for the poor ; and he has discussed the matter in *The Silver Box*. He is worried by those cohesions of caste which sometimes run counter to truth and justice ; and he has brought them out for an airing in *Loyalties*. The problem of the land is a grave one. English agriculture is in a bad way, and so is the population engaged in it : sometimes model landlords are the worst of all, because the very principles which make them exemplary lead them also to be narrow and tyrannous. Mr. Galsworthy goes into this in *The Freelands*. Industrial unrest is a serious business. There are faults and obstinacies on both sides which, as is demonstrated in *Strife*, bring misery to innocent women and children. Then there is a whole series of discussions of the problem of marriage and divorce. Mr. Galsworthy is passionate in his repeated protests against the fact that a woman may continue to be regarded as the property of a man whom she has ceased to love. This situation provides the most poignant element in the best of all his books ; and his attitude towards it is summed up at the end of *The Forsyte Saga*, where Young Jolyon and Irene prevent their son, Jon, from marrying Fleur, the daughter of the man whose property Irene was once held to be. Young Jolyon writes to his son :—

" I don't wish to write harshly of Soames Forsyte. I don't think harshly of him. I have long been sorry for him ; perhaps I was sorry even then. As the world judges she was in error, he within his rights. He loved her—in his way. *She was his property*. That is the view he holds of life—of human feelings and hearts—property. It's not his fault—so was he born. To me it is a view that has always been abhorrent—so was I born ! Knowing you as I do, I feel it cannot be otherwise than abhorrent to you."

This rises naturally enough out of the situation ; but it is something more than an element in the story. It is a demand, a propagandist demand, coming from the author himself, that something which has been should cease to be. This fact, if it were not apparent, might be proved by the frequent cropping up of the same situation, in various forms, throughout Mr. Galsworthy's works. In *The Dark Flower*, Mark Lennan, Olive Cramier and her husband repeat almost exactly the grouping of Philip Bosinney, Irene Forsyte and her husband, though here the *dénouement* comes by the death of the wife, not the lover. In *The Fugitive* Clare Dedmond runs away from a husband who does not appreciate the beauty of sunsets or music, but nevertheless appreciates her personal beauty only too well. Courtier, in *The Patrician*, pleads in similar terms the right to liberty of Audrey Noel, whose husband, from whom she is separated, will not divorce her, though he does not persecute her, and whose lover, Lord Miltoun, is prevented, by conscientious scruples, from taking her as his mistress. Only in *The Country House* does a sugges- tion appear that there is another and not so admirable type of woman who falls in love and marries and falls out of love and demands freedom. Mrs. Bellew is represented as doing equal harm, by her lightness, to her husband and her lover ; and the advocate of liberty in this case is made to look something of a fool.

I have laid stress on this theme, and Mr. Galsworthy's treatment of it, partly because it bulks so largely in his work as to seem almost an obsession, partly because, more than any of the other causes he has argued, it shows him as a deliberate and undisguised critic of modern institutions and of modern ways of thinking about them. He is definitely a man who wants certain things done, certain things changed ; and, under one aspect, his novels and plays are illustration of his arguments on these points. It used to be the fashion to raise an uproar against an imaginative artist who used his imagination for such a purpose. To me, I confess, it has never seemed that there was such a dearth of imaginative literature as to make criminal the diversion of a certain amount of power, which might have created a little more, into the service of a specific reform : only the artist himself can judge what is his duty in this respect. But it may be doubted whether any such choice ever presented itself to Mr. Galsworthy. His propagandist strain is something native and ineradicable in him. It is one of the two motives from which he writes, and it is generally almost equal, sometimes, indeed, superior in strength to that which must, from the point of view of pure literature, be considered the better motive. For if we take the "criticism of life" at the false value which its somewhat clumsy phrasing has invited, then the proper motive of pure literature, a motive which is not lacking in Mr. Galsworthy's work, is the appreciation of life. That he does write from this motive is sufficiently proved by the remarkable fact that his upholders of established institutions, the very persons against whom, from his other motive, his lance is constantly directed, are generally the most artistically satisfying and often even personally the most attractive of his characters. To this fact I must later return : at present I leave it as convincing evidence that the artist, however intermixed with another personality, is alive enough in Mr. Galsworthy.

That other personality, however, does exist side by side with the artist and does hamper him. This is nowhere more visible than in the plays. Mr. Galsworthy has somewhere said that it may be that, whether from inexperience or from want of aptitude, he moves with a sort of cramped action on the stage. This is not obvious, to me at least. *The Silver Box*, *Justice*, *Loyalties*—to take three pieces at random—are excellent examples of dramatic carpentry, which successfully hold the attention of an audience : it is less with their execution than with the ideas expressed by them that it is possible to quarrel.

The Silver Box and *Justice* are probably the plays which have earned Mr. Galsworthy his reputation of being the most thoroughgoing realist among English writers ; and these pieces are undoubtedly influenced by the German realists, such as Arno Holz and Gerhart Hauptmann. Ibsen, in so far as he was a realist at all, was a realist of the middle classes ; and he always had a plot, told a story, and dealt with exceptional people. The Germans, with *Vor Sonnenaufgang* and *Fuhrmann Henschel*, took a header into the life of the masses. Moreover, it was their aim to illustrate the texture of ordinary life by means of typical examples. This was also Mr. Galsworthy's aim in these two plays. In the first of them he takes an undistinguished police-court case and says in effect : Now let us see what really did happen. According to Mr. Galsworthy's report of his researches what really did happen was this. Jack Barthwick, the young and foolish son of a respectable Liberal member of Parliament, after a night out with a doubtful young woman, steals her purse in a fit of drunken spite and returns home incapable of using his latchkey. A drunken loiterer named Jones helps him in, and, after a drink or two, and after hearing Jack boast about how he has " scored off " his mistress, makes off with the purse and with a silver box to score *him* off—Jack having previously drunkenly invited him to " take anything you like." Now it so happens that Mrs. Jones is employed as a charwoman in the house of the Barthwicks, and suspicion falls on her of having stolen the box. A detective is sent to her lodgings and finds it there, and she is arrested. Jones confesses to the theft and gives himself up. Meanwhile, Jack's young woman has called at the house to reclaim her money, and thus her existence and the affair of the purse have become known to the scandalised senior Barthwick. The last scene is in the police-court ; and, thanks to the adroitness of Barthwick's solicitor, Jones gets one month's hard labour without the whole story being told. Thus it is shown that there is one law for the rich and respectable and another for the poor and suspect.

On all this there is one first comment to be made, that, the purse having been found on Jones and mentioned in court, it is unlikely that the magistrate would have altogether suppressed Jones's cry when Jack is in the witness-box, " You ask *'im* what made *'im* take the——" However, it might have happened. There is a similar hardship in *Justice*, where Falder's plea of the temptation under which he committed forgery is turned against him by the judge. This is another typical sample of life. Falder, who is anything but a real criminal by nature, is led into crime by weakness and circumstances, suffers in prison out of all proportion to his guilt, is unable to recover his place in the world, and finally leaves the world altogether by way of a high staircase, down which he throws himself.

These are typical examples of life, so Mr. Galsworthy would have us believe. But of course, they are not ; and of course, a Forsyte might say, they are the hard cases which make good law. These plays do call attention to certain possible abuses of our social system. They proclaim that in certain cases the rich have a legal advantage over the poor and that in certain cases our antiquated penology confirms in crime those who have entered that career only by an accident. But, because they exaggerate, they are not good art ; and, because they exaggerate, they are dangerous argument. When Mr. Galsworthy writes for the theatre, his humanitarian sentiment runs away with him. These plays do not present typical, everyday cases : therefore they are faulty as illustrations of political or sociological arguments. They do not show under an extreme strain human nature at its highest : therefore they are faulty as art. Jones and Falder are unhappy accidents : they cannot thoroughly engage our sympathies. Jones is neither the ordinary Jones who walks our streets, nor yet Macbeth. Falder, an insignificant person, is promoted to high suffering by chance, a chance which does not visit one person in ten thousand. But, knowing this, we cannot take much interest in him as a typical case ; and he, being what he is, cannot to any great extent arouse our sympathy with him for his own sake. Mr. Galsworthy falls, here, between two stools. We sympathise with Macbeth, we *appreciate* him, because he is a high expression of human nature under an extreme strain. We might sympathise with Falder if we could think he was Everyman. But he is not, and Mr. Galsworthy does not succeed in making us think that he is.

In all this there is some suggestion that Mr. Galsworthy plays with loaded dice, and I do not find in myself any anxiety to escape from making that imputation. Whether one says " loaded dice " or " debating tricks," it comes to much the same thing ; and I contend, quite simply, that in his plays Mr. Galsworthy does not tell the truth. Let us take the third of the pieces which I have named as examples of his really admirable stage-craft, the piece called *Loyalties*. This play filled a London theatre for some hundreds of performances ; and as a person who voluntarily went to see it for a second time I can testify that it is an interesting and exciting play. But its intellectual structure is exceedingly flimsy. Ferdy de Levis, staying in a country house, has a thousand pounds in notes stolen from his bedroom. He, loyal to the traditions of his race, wants his money back. His host, Charles Winsor, loyal to the traditions of country houses, does not want a scandal in his own. Charles Winsor and his associates, loyal to the traditions of caste, cannot bear to believe that one of themselves has stolen the money from this damned Jew. The matter comes into Court in the form of an action for slander ; and conclusive evidence is brought to the notice of Ronald Dancy's solicitor that Ronald Dancy, as de Levis believed, is the thief. The solicitor's personal sympathies are all with his client; but he has his loyalty to the traditions of his profession. The case is thrown up; a warrant is issued; Dancy shoots himself. This clockwork rabbit manœuvres about the nursery floor with delightful vivacity; but, I submit, the thing would not have happened thus in real life. At the beginning an experienced and influential member of the Winsor and Dancy set obtains certain evidence which convinces him of Dancy's guilt; and though he might have attempted to hush the matter up, it is in the last degree unlikely that he would have attempted to burke it by the methods which General Canynge uses with Ferdy de Levis. General Canynge would, in my judgment, have said to Dancy: "Look here, any one of us is liable to go mad once in a while. Tell me honestly, did you do it? If so, give me the money and I'll get it back to de Levis somehow, and we can forget it." But what General Canynge does say in the play, after forming his suspicion and communicating it to Winsor, is recorded thus:—

"CANYNGE (*with cold decision*): Young Dancy was an officer and is a gentleman; this insinuation is pure supposition, and you must not make it. Do you understand me?

"DE LEVIS: My tongue is still mine, General, if my money isn't.

"CANYNGE (*unmoved*): Must not. You're a member of three Clubs, you want to be a member of a fourth. No one who makes such an insinuation against a fellow-guest in a country house, except on absolute proof, can do so without complete ostracism. Have we your word to say nothing?

"DE LEVIS: Social blackmail? H'm!

"CANYNGE: Not at all—simple warning. If

you consider it necessary in your interests to start this scandal—no matter how, we shall consider it necessary in ours to dissociate ourselves completely from one who so recklessly disregards the unwritten code."

To be quite frank, I don't believe it. I believe that Mr. Galsworthy, touching this real problem of "loyalties," has made an unreal, though theatrically effective, debating case of it. Here though, as elsewhere, he is the friend of the under-dog. In this play his sympathies are with de Levis, the man robbed, and with Dancy, the man betrayed by his temperament and by the foolish loyalties of his friends. To be on the side of the underdog is, with him, a real passion ; and had he had any gift of lyrical expression his work might have taken on another, a more poetical and ideal poise. But, as his one volume of verse shows, this gift has been denied to him : and his passion for the oppressed shows itself more often in special pleading than in lyrical outbursts.

The plays are almost all efforts of special pleading. They are arguments in favour of particular cases much more exclusively than are the novels. And, of course, special pleading in the theatre is a difficult thing to make effective. The restrained and realistic method employed by Mr. Galsworthy succeeds as a rule only in making him seem feebly well-meaning. One catches in most of his pieces as it were an echo of Mr. Barthwick's in *The Silver Box* : "If we are not able to do much for them we are bound to have the greatest sympathy with the poor." And tendencious works of which the upshot is like this do not greatly stir the blood. The fact seems to be that Mr. Galsworthy can only rarely use the better, the life-giving element in his talent on the stage. He is not clumsy, not deficient in craftsmanship, but when he enters the theatre he leaves an essential part of himself behind.

A critic who knew him only in the theatre might be pardoned for thinking him only a well-intentioned and mildly despairing humanitarian, for thinking that Mr. Max Beerbohm's amusing parody in the *Christmas Garland* covered all the ground. It will be remembered that Adrian Berridge says to his wife, during their breakfast of boiled eggs and toast, when she guiltily desires to throw bread-crumbs to the birds outside, "Jacynth, don't you remember that long talk we had last winter, after the annual meeting of the Feathered Friends' League, and how we agreed that these sporadic doles could do no real good—must even degrade the birds who received them—and that we had no right to meddle in what ought to be done by collective action of the State?" Mr. Galsworthy has fallen many times under the suspicion of belonging to that bleakest and least attractive of all human types—the ascetic who is not a fanatic, the ascetic who leads that life through deficiency, not excess, of temperament. The judgment is correct in so far as he is sometimes an ascetic and never a fanatic. But he is not always an ascetic, and it is important to state what, so far as I know, has never yet been remarked, that few English authors have written so well and with so deep a gusto on the subject of food. There is, to be sure, often an ironic purpose, and an ironic flavour in his description of an elaborate menu. Swithin Forsyte, giving the last touches to his dinner party, says, "Adolf, the least touch of the West India when you come to the ham." It is satirical, but the author's pen seems involuntarily to vibrate in sympathy. No ascetic, whether by excess or deficiency, could have imagined that speech. Then there is the tremendous dinner-party where were present Soames and Irene Forsyte, June Forsyte, and Philip Bosinney. None of them enjoyed their food ; but Mr. Galsworthy and his readers do. The dinner consisted of soup, " excellent, if a little thick," " a fine fresh sole from Dover," " cutlets pink-frilled about the legs," spring chicken and salad, asparagus, an apple charlotte, French olives and caviare, and German plums. At the end " Egyptian cigarettes were handed in a silver box," and " Turkish coffee followed in enamelled cups "; and the brandy which Soames pressed Bosinney to take was " pale and old." Altogether an admirable meal for the hot, breathless evening on which it took place, and it seems a pity that so little of it was eaten by those for whom it was provided. Then there is the wine which Old Jolyon offers to Irene when he entertains her unexpectedly at dinner :—

" There, in the wine-cellar, was a hock worth at least two pounds a bottle, a Steinberg Cabinet, better than any Johannisberg that ever went down throat ; a wine of perfect bouquet, sweet as a nectarine—nectar indeed ! He got a bottle out, handling it like a baby, and holding it level to the light, to look. Enshrined in its coat of dust, that mellow-coloured, slender-necked bottle gave him deep pleasure. Three years to settle down again since the move from town—ought to be in prime condition ! Thirty-five years ago he had bought it—thank God he had kept his palate, and earned the right to drink it. She would appreciate this ; not a spice of acidity in a dozen. He wiped the bottle, drew the cork with his own hands, put his nose down, inhaled its perfume, and went back to the music-room."

Or there is Sylvanus Heythorp's last dinner in *The Stoic*, a masterpiece of luxury and tragedy. Old Heythorp, brought to the end at last after a magnificent and piratical career, determines to commit suicide by eating and drinking all that medical advice had pronounced to be most dangerous to him. The evening began with a hot bath in water impregnated with pine essence ; and it ended with death. All that went between, from the oysters which opened the meal to the brandy which gave the *coup de grâce*, was perfect of its kind. This was euthanasia such as Mr. Wells's future never imagined.

Now it will be observed that none of these exhibitions of gustatory expertise is gratuitously introduced : I do not suppose that Mr. Galsworthy will ever write a cookery-book or a handbook for gourmets. Every meal in his works (and there are unusually many) has its due place in a patent exposition of character and motive. And it may seem that in insisting on this point I am forcing on Mr. Galsworthy a grossness which is altogether my own. But I contend, in the first place, that, for whatever purpose he uses these remarkable collations, Mr. Galsworthy could not have invented them without himself taking a genuine delight in good food and drink, and, in the second place, that this emotion is symptomatic of the element in his talent which enables him to write novels of the first rank. To return to a phrase I have used earlier in this essay—he *appreciates* life.

Three out of the four examples given above

come from the dispersed and irregular work to which its author gives the title of *The Forsyte Saga*. In this title there is an element of an irony, which is not in Mr. Galsworthy's happiest vein, though he knows the objections to which it is open, and has defended it, but which is not worth disputing here. The title is not of great importance, though perhaps that given to the first section of the work, *The Man of Property*, might most suitably have described the whole. Property is in our community a magical word, a centre of all the fighting of modern civilisation. Mr. Galsworthy revolts against its implications ; Mr. Belloc holds that the instinct for it is something instinctive and rightly ineradicable in human nature. But Mr. Galsworthy is too good an artist not to realise the richness of life, of living power, which has, during thousands and thousands of years, built up this institution and still maintains it. The Forsytes are, for him, symbols of the property-holding class, and " the figure of Irene, never, as the reader may possibly have noticed, present, except through the senses of other characters, is a concretion of disturbing Beauty impinging on a possessive world."

The general character of Mr. Galsworthy's work in fiction might be exemplified from other books ; but this is, I think, immeasurably the best of all, his most weighty, and *a* most weighty, contribution to modern literature. It enjoys one considerable advantage over most of the others : there is in it no *raisonneur* on the side of liberty. It must be confessed that Courtier, in *The Patrician*, and Gregory Vigil in *The Country House* grow a little tedious with their well-intentioned harangues. But in the *Forsyte Saga* we have the Forsytes on the one side and Irene, unconscious, involuntary symbol of a whole element of life, on the other. Irene is indisputably Mr. Galsworthy's best " concretion " of that element in life which does not uphold established institutions, and will not submit to them. She is magic, she is beauty, she is love ; and, as her creator remarks, she is " never present except through the senses of other characters." Or, as M. André Chevrillon says in his admirable essay on Mr. Galsworthy, she and her lover remain in the wings while their shadows are projected on to the stage.

Bosinney's shadow, even so, is thin and a little unconvincing ; but Irene's shadow is a real creation. She is not merely the figment of a progressive humanitarian, a stick with which the reactionaries may be satisfactorily beaten. She is a form of life, an embodiment of that sexual attraction which utterly transcends sex : hers is, indeed, the modern counterpart of the face which launched a thousand ships, and it is capable of burning the perhaps not topless, but very respectable, and therefore much safer, towers which house all the members of the tribe of Forsyte. In her, for once, Mr. Galsworthy succeeds in presenting a poetic, an almost mythical, embodiment of that spirit of liberty and beauty which elsewhere he has to show in harder, less sympathetic and less convincing terms. Because he has here done this, the *Forsyte Saga* has a balance and completeness which no other of his books approaches.

Oddly enough, he never falls short in his presentation of the characters whom he attacks. With the timid, the respectable, the self-satisfied, he deals confidently and convincingly. It might even be said without unfairness that he lavishes on them more of the pains which proclaim love than on the persons whose causes he manifestly champions. He has perhaps given to no portrait more careful and affectionate labour than he has bestowed on the portrait of Soames Forsyte. Of this figure he says, in a very important preface, which has already been quoted :—

"One has noticed that readers, as they wade on through the salt waters of the Saga, are inclined more and more to pity Soames, and to think that in doing so they are in revolt against the mood of the creator. Far from it ! He, too, pities Soames ; the tragedy of his life is the very simple, uncontrollable tragedy of being unloveable, without quite a thick enough skin to be thoroughly unconscious of the fact."

This is true, and because Mr. Galsworthy creates, as all true artists do, beyond his consciousness of what he has done, it is equally true of the Soames of *The Man of Property* and the Soames of *To Let.* But between *The Man of Property*, first published in 1906, and *To Let*, first published in 1920, there has been some sort of a change in the mind which first imagined Soames. That figure sprang potentially complete out of Mr. Galsworthy's mind, no one can say that there is any inconsistency between the first Soames and the last. But Mr. Galsworthy's intellect and judgment have undergone a natural change during the intervening fourteen years. The wheel has come full circle, which, in a work of art, is a desirable thing to happen ; and now Mr. Galsworthy's love of Soames, always inevitable (for it is a law that the creator must sooner or later love his creations), is to the fullest extent apparent instead of being concealed. The *Forsyte Saga* leaves Irene in the possession of relatively satisfactory memories ; but Soames's life has been to the end a life of almost unrelieved tragedy. Mr. Galsworthy loveth whom he chasteneth ; and this is a mark of the truly imaginative artist.[1]

The balance of this work is very nearly triangular. In Irene we have the apex of the triangle, the struggle of liberty against the fetters imposed on it. At one side of the base sits Soames, the tragic protagonist of established institutions, and at the other, Swithin, the comic relief. (I must own to finding both Old and Young Jolyon a trifle too liable to sentimentality to rank on the same plane with the persons I have named.) And Swithin Forsyte is an interesting piece of invention. In a story which Mr. Galsworthy, for excellent reasons, has not thought fit to bind up with the rest (but it can be found in the volume called *Villa Rubein*), we find him as a young man making love to, almost marrying, an Hungarian young girl of wandering temperament and revolutionary connections. When he first appears in the canon we learn that :—

" Swithin had indeed an impatience of simplicity, a love of ormolu, which had always stamped him amongst his associates as a man of great, if somewhat luxurious taste ; and out of the knowledge that no one could possibly enter his rooms without perceiving him to be a man of wealth he had derived a solid and prolonged happiness such as perhaps no other circumstance in life had afforded him.

" Since his retirement from house agency, a profession deplorable in his estimation, especially

[1] More years have gone by and, as one knew he must, Mr. Galsworthy has continued the story of the Forsytes. But the *White Monkey* and *Silver Spoon* only reinforce my argument.

as to its auctioneering department, he had abandoned himself to naturally aristocratic tastes.

"The perfect luxury of his latter days had embedded him like a fly in sugar; and his mind, where very little took place from morning till night, was the junction of two curiously opposite emotions, a lingering and sturdy satisfaction that he had made his own way and his own fortune, and a sense that a man of his distinction should never have been allowed to soil his mind with work."

Swithin is, whether Mr. Galsworthy means him to be or not, the justification of the old way of life. How he enjoys himself! He has his well-furnished rooms, his nearly perfect servant, his horses, his dinner-parties; when he dies, dazedly contemplating the bubbles in a forbidden glass of champagne, who ever died more happily? He is one of the best three of Mr. Galsworthy's creations; and, like Mr. Galsworthy's loving care in the description of meals, he illustrates what is here most necessary to be illustrated.

The quality shown in the affectionate, appreciative characterisation of Swithin is precisely that which informs the whole chronicle of the Forsytes and makes it not only Mr. Galsworthy's best novel but also one of the very few good and typical novels of our time. The one volume edition contains a genealogical table which dismays the intending reader, and is practically useless to him who has read. It may be interesting on occasion to refer to it and confirm one's recollection of the precise relationship between Young Nicholas and Giles Hayman, characters who cut no great figure in the story; but the impression which the whole work gives of a large and various family, flourishing and alive as a group, is more valuable than the power to pin down these details.

Mr. Galsworthy succeeds in giving this impression, succeeds in making his family live and flourish over a period of some thirty-five years, just because here his appreciation of life as it is triumphs over his desire to alter things, passes into the contemplative ecstasy which is the true source of creative art. In almost all his other works, even the novels, the ghost of Mr. Barthwick sooner or later passes across the scene, muttering without conviction that, " if we are not able to do much for them we are bound to have the greatest sympathy with the poor." This sentence is an almost perfect summary of *The Island Pharisees*, where the reader flags on through some hundreds of pages, not surprised that Dick Shelton, with his vague, undirected humanitarianism, should be unable to hold his Antonia, but very much surprised that he should want to hold her. It echoes even in *The Country House*, to me easily the second of Mr. Galsworthy's novels : though Gregory Vigil is disappointed in his championship of Helen Bellew, it is not clear that any satire on his ineffectual idealism is intended. In *The Dark Flower* this note is absent ; but *The Dark Flower* is, for other reasons, an unsatisfactory book. Here the ghost which crosses the scene is that of Irene ; and she crosses twice, first as Anna Stormer, then as Olive Cramier, perhaps even a third time, as a ghost of what Irene might have been if her conflict with the accepted had begun at a much earlier age, under the name of Nell Dromore. This narrative contains excellent scenes and beautiful passages ; and if it were a series of preliminary sketches for Irene instead of having been written some seven years after *The Man of Property*, it would be interesting. But Mark Lennan, the hero, is a failure, a stick.

Mr. Galsworthy's heroes are generally failures when he lets them get into the middle of the stage. Apparently he is a fair-minded man who has by an intellectual decision adopted the humanitarian and progressive side ; and, as fair-minded men often do, he has studied, and states, the case of his antagonists with more curiosity and gusto than he gives to his own. Hence it is his Philistines and reactionaries, like Swithin Forsyte and George Pendyce, his ducks who are lame because of their own unlovely temperaments, like Soames Forsyte, his piratical pests of society, like the unscrupulous old robber, Sylvanus Heythorp, who dominate his work and give it its salt and its vigour. But these characters are, after all, more frequent in modern life and often more interesting than the humanitarians and progressives. Mr. Galsworthy has to his credit a gallery of them, coolly observed and described with exquisite precision. Luckily in one case he found the exact balance which enabled him to get the very best out of his talent. In writing the separate parts of *The Forsyte Saga*, he pursued the development of the struggle between the forces symbolised by Soames and the forces symbolised by Irene long enough for his talent to grow mellow. And the more he loved Soames, the nearer he came to an understanding of that unhappy figure, the better did the balance become. The essence of such a struggle is that our sympathies should be engaged on both sides ; and by the time that he has reached about the thousandth page the reader feels either that he has attained the state of knowledge in which judgment is suspended or that else he must assume towards these puppets the prerogative of judgment which with real persons is God's alone. To have brought an invented situation to such a point is no mean feat. By the way, Mr. Galsworthy has set down much valuable and vivacious social observation and satire—enough to give enduring life to his book. But he has done more than this. The struggle he thus describes is an eternal struggle; and his interest in it, in its eternal aspect, has overcome his interest in its merely temporal details. This book at least fulfils the conditions of great art : the persons in it are recognisable human beings, true to the requirements of time and place, but they are also symbols of forces which will continue in battle until human nature has evolved into some form which we should not be able to recognise at all.

Mr. D. H. Lawrence

MR. D. H. LAWRENCE lives at the bottom of a dark pit. He is always trying to clamber out of it ; and sometimes he thinks that he has succeeded. He is, however, invariably wrong when he thinks so : his fingers slip on the brink, he slides back, and the struggle begins all over again. He believes, too, that the whole of the human race is living at the bottom of the same pit. Perhaps he is right. But the question whether he is right or not is one that, sooner or later, when we consider his work, we must ask ourselves : he himself does not allow us to evade that question. The persons of his imagination are persons in ordinary circumstances : farmers, colliers, elementary school teachers, and the like, living in the unfamiliar but not specially romantic or legendary coal district of Nottinghamshire. But in their physical experiences they are a little, and in their mental and spiritual experiences, more than a little, abnormal. The ostensible mode of all Mr. Lawrence's books, whether in prose or in verse, is what we are accustomed to call realistic. These are people who get up and go to bed, who talk, sometimes, in a recognisable dialect, who wash and eat and have holes in their socks. But—

" Swiftly in a flame that drenched down her body like fluid lightning and gave her a perfect, unutterable consummation, unutterable satisfaction, she brought down the ball of jewel stone with all her force, crash on his head. But her fingers were in the way and deadened the blow. Nevertheless, down went his head on the table on which his book lay, the stone slid aside and over his ear, it was one convulsion of pure bliss for her, lit up by the crushed pain of her fingers. But it was not somehow complete. She lifted her arm high to aim once more, straight down on the head that lay dazed on the table. She must smash it, it must be smashed before her ecstasy was consummated, fulfilled for ever. A thousand lives, a thousand deaths mattered nothing now, only the fulfilment of this perfect ecstasy.

" She was not swift, she could only move slowly. A strong spirit in him woke him and made him lift his face and twist to look at her. Her arm was raised, the hand clasping the ball of lapis lazuli. It was her left hand, he realised again with horror that she was left-handed. Hurriedly, with a burrowing motion, he covered his head under the thick volume of Thucydides, and the blow came down, almost breaking his neck and shattering his heart."

This scene takes place in an English country-house, in the boudoir of Hermione, who is a cultivated member of the governing classes. She strikes the blow ; the recipient of it is Rupert Birkin, an inspector of schools, who is sitting there reading while she writes her letters. When it is over, he goes out, takes off all his clothes, runs about in the rain, and feels better. The invention of the scene is strange enough, but one detail in it is even stranger. Why should Rupert, at a moment when one might have expected him to be startled and frightened into unsubtle normality—why should he, just then, experience horror at being reminded of Hermione's left-handedness ?

Let us take another example—this time from Mr. Lawrence's verse of an earlier period, from the poem called *Snapdragon* :—

" She turned her flushed face to me for the glint
Of a moment. 'See,' she laughed, 'if you also
Can make them yawn ?' I put my hand to the dint
In the flower's throat, and the flower gaped wide with woe.
She watched, she went of a sudden intensely still,
She watched my hand to see what it would fulfil.

" I pressed the wretched, throttled flower between
My fingers, till its head lay back, its fangs
Poised at her. Like a weapon my hand was white and keen,
And I held the choked flower-serpent in its pangs
Of mordant anguish, till she ceased to laugh,
Until her pride's flag, smitten, cleaved down to the staff.

" She hid her face, she murmured between her lips
The low word 'Don't.' . . ."

Now such a symbolic condensation of an emotional crisis is less unexpected in verse than in prose ; but it is typical of what Mr. Lawrence constantly does in both. Even when verse deals with every-day life we do not ask of it that the details shall be verisimilitudinous, we expect it to go beyond the larger surface and give us the smaller core. But in novels, more particularly where the author says : " She wore a dress of dark-blue silky stuff, with ruches of blue and green linen lace in the neck and sleeves ; and she had emerald-green stockings," we expect all the events and details to be invented, however they may be arranged, strictly with a view to probability. It is something of a shock when we find they are not. Now Mr. Lawrence does nothing to soften this shock. He is, on the surface, neither a romantic nor a symbolist. He seemed even, to some of his early reviewers, to be a painter of the manners of the Midlands, not incomparable with Mr. Arnold Bennett. Perhaps the Nottingham colliery district of which he wrote was so unfamiliar that London critics were at first ready to believe of it almost anything they were told. Mr. Bennett indeed had often insisted on both the incredibility and the strict truth of his pictures of the Five Towns. These pictures were not, perhaps, so amazing as he would have had us believe ; but critics are impressionable creatures, or they would not be critics. They came, very likely, to think that another dispensation obtained north of the Chilterns, in which southern standards of probability must be applied with caution. But gradually it began to be obvious that if one were to take the realistic texture of Mr. Lawrence's work, whether in prose or in verse, at its face-value, one would have to conclude that it is peopled with ill-mannered, hypersensitive and hysterical lunatics; one would have to begin and end with the judgment that human beings do not talk like this, do not behave in this way.

It is a first sign of Mr. Lawrence's quality that he does not allow us, he has never allowed any one, to come to such a conclusion. To-day we are rather apt, indeed, to be over-impressed by obscurity. We cannot help remembering that earlier generations thought not only Browning but even Tennyson to be unintelligible ; and, with this recollection in our minds, we go about in modern literature a good deal too ready to buy any pig in a poke, because to us the existence of the poke connotes the superlative goodness of the pig. But Mr. Lawrence's obscurity has a different effect. Here we feel that the author is doing his best and that some of the effort towards comprehension must come from ourselves. Here is work which will perhaps appear to a later generation as lucid as most of Browning does to us, work which, like the famous sonata of Marcel Proust's Vinteuil, must gradually create its own understanding audience. If we can take a few steps in that direction, we shall have done something on which we may congratulate ourselves. But, before we do so, we must renounce the pleasure of objecting that members of the English governing classes do not beat school-inspectors over the head with lapis lazuli paper-weights. We must remember, to begin with, that Mr. Lawrence's work has enough obvious and normal virtues to prove him not to be an idiot.

His work is considerable in extent for a career which began no longer than twelve years ago. It consists of seven substantial novels, a volume of short stories, a volume of long-short stories, two plays, four collections of verse, and two books of travel. Not all of this bulk is equally good ; but none of it is trivial or even can be described as having been lightly undertaken. Mr. Lawrence sometimes writes badly : he seems never to write with anything less than the full intensity of which he is capable. And it must be remembered, in computing his total production, that between *The Rainbow* in 1915 and *The Lost Girl* in 1920, he published no novel. This was no doubt due to the unfortunate suppression of *The Rainbow*.

The important part of this work is to be found in the novels. But would Mr. Lawrence, under other conditions than those which obtain to-day, have chosen the medium of the novel? Has he been altogether wise in doing so? These questions are difficult to answer. One is inclined at first to maintain that neither his material nor his particular talent for expression is suited to this form, and that, but for the tyranny which rules our literature and decrees that any man who wishes to earn a living in it must be either novelist or reviewer, he would have chosen some other. And yet *The Trespasser* at least, his second novel, apart from the magnificent descriptive passages which it contains, is excellent in form, a well-told, compact, and shapely story. And, of the scenes which one remembers, how many could have been rendered in any other medium?

Mr. Lawrence's novels are mostly shapeless, ragged, diffuse. But for the example of *The Trespasser* one would be tempted to say that his narrative sense is incapable of standing by him for above half a dozen pages: even his short stories are often amorphous lumps. *The Rainbow* rambles on through three generations. Each generation is elaborately painted in, only to be discarded when the next is old enough for the author to take interest in it. From the point of view of telling a story, this book contains more wasted labour than almost any other I know. Tom Brangwen might well say that if he was so soon to be done for, he wondered what he was begun for. But he leaves the book in one of the best of Mr. Lawrence's scenes. He is drowned, while a little drunk, in an unexpected flood ; and the reader does not forget his death. His adopted daughter, Anna, and her husband, William Brangwen, fade out far more ignominiously, only to make belated and ghostly appearances in *Women in Love*. It is Ursula to whom the rainbow appears, Ursula on whom the full force of the book is concentrated ; and Ursula is not born till more than a third of the book is done, does not develop a personality till it is half-way through. When she does, Mr. Lawrence throws aside the characters on whom he has spent so many pains and whom he has not completely explained, and turns to her.

There is not, in all this, any suggestion of subtlety or premeditation : one does feel on the contrary, quite definitely, that Mr. Lawrence is making it all up as he goes on, leaving one page to suggest the next, penetrating to the hearts of his characters only one page in advance of his readers. In more demonstrable ways, he is almost insolent in his carelessness. *The White Peacock*, though it is told in the first person, contains scenes of which the narrator could not possibly have had any knowledge. In *The Rainbow*, events are huddled together or dwelt on with no regard to the symmetry or the substantiation of the story. Ursula and Skrebensky have indulged in a passionate and secret love affair for a considerable time. Then :—

" He could not come again to Nottingham until the end of April. Then he persuaded her to go with him for a week-end to a friend's house near Oxford. By this time they were engaged. He had written to her father, and the thing was settled. He bought her an emerald ring, of which she was very proud."

Now to such persons as these are, as Mr. Lawrence has conceived them, the public avowal of a mutual relation must have been an important event; nothing is gained, something is lost by this brusque dismissal of it. In another writer it might have been a yawn, in Mr. Lawrence it is the hunter's eagerness, but it is not good narrative, anywhere.

It is not incapacity, it is merely the author's striving after something which occupies his mind more than comely and lucid story-telling. But to say this might suggest that Mr. Lawrence altogether neglects the flesh and bone of the novel, that he emaciates it to a gaunt ugliness in his search for something of the spirit. This, however, would not be true. There are few living writers more capable of clothing what they imagine in solid and beautiful flesh. To be sure, he can write badly, with his eye anywhere but on the object, as in the instance of the rabbit.

"And suddenly the rabbit, which had been crouching as if it were a flower, so still and soft, burst into life. Round and round the court it went, as if shot from a gun, round and round like a furry meteorite, in a tense hard circle that seemed to bind their brains. They all stood in amazement, smiling uncannily, as if the rabbit were obeying some unknown incantation. Round and round it flew, on the grass under the old red walls like a storm."

Three similes to describe one rabbit, and two of them as unsuited to the purpose as can be imagined.

Indeed, in the tumult of his later work Mr. Lawrence's impressionistic power of rendering material things and scenes does appear to have lost some of its certainty. He is feverishly determined to render the half apprehended, almost wholly incommunicable mental states of his characters and when he is describing their surroundings, distracted by this, he fumbles, he repeats himself, he blurs the image by attempting to infuse into it something he has failed to express elsewhere. Perhaps this old power is one of the things he must, or feels he must, throw over in the pursuit of his new goal. But his earlier books had extraordinarily full, rich, and vivid backgrounds. As one turns over the pages of *The White Peacock*, one is astonished to find how many descriptive passages there are and how warmly they glow with life. As one reads the book, one hardly observes their profusion, for they are a true background. Mr. Lawrence is never irrelevant or self-conscious in the use of his descriptive powers. But when one looks for them they yield themselves, separable and lovely. Here is the episode of the keeper's funeral—

"Till the heralds come—till the heralds wave like shadows in the bright air, crying, lamenting, fretting for ever. Rising and falling and circling round and round, the slow-waving peewits cry and complain, and lift their broad wings in sorrow. They stoop suddenly to the ground, the lapwings, then in another throb of anguish and protest, they swing up again, offering a glistening white breast to the sunlight, to deny it in black shadows, then a glisten of green, and all the time crying and crying in despair.

"The pheasants are frightened into cover, they

run and dart through the hedge. The cold cock must fly in his haste, spread himself on his streaming plumes, and sail into the wood's security.

" There is a cry in answer to the peewits, echoing louder and stronger the lamentation of the lapwings, a wail which hushes the birds. The men come over the brow of the hill, slowly, with the old squire walking tall and straight in front ; six bowed men bearing the coffin on their shoulders, treading heavily and cautiously, under the great weight of the glistening white coffin ; six men following behind, ill at ease, waiting their turn for the burden. You can see the red handkerchiefs knotted round their throats, and their shirt-fronts blue and white between the open waistcoats. The coffin is of new unpolished wood, gleaming and glistening in the sunlight ; the men who carry it remember all their lives after the smell of new warm elm-wood.

" Again a loud cry from the hill-top. The woman has followed thus far, the big, shapeless woman, and she cries with loud cries after the white coffin as it descends the hill, and the children that cling to her skirts weep aloud, and are not to be hushed by the other woman, who bends over them, but does not form one of the group. How the crying frightens the birds and the rabbits and the lambs ; away these run to their mothers. But the peewits are not frightened, they add their notes to the sorrow ; they circle after the white, retreating coffin, they circle round the woman ; it is they who for ever keen the sorrows of this world. They are like priests in their robes, more black than white, more grief than hope, driving endlessly round and round, turning, lifting, falling and crying always in mournful desolation, repeating their last syllables like the broken accents of despair."

I wish I could continue the quotation to the end of the chapter, to the narrator's return home :—

"The house was quiet and complacent ; it was peopled with ghosts again ; but the ghosts had only come to enjoy the warm place once more, carrying sunshine in their arms and scattering it through the dusk of gloomy rooms."

The thing is perfect of its kind. It is just because among the novelists who come after Mr. Hardy and Mr. Conrad so few can do so much, so few appear even to want to do it, that the modern novel is the rather arid and unsatisfying thing which we feel it to be.

In *The Trespasser*, again, the scene blends with the story, and there are unforgettably beautiful passages of description. After this the background is not so pervasive or so consistent in excellence, though Mr. Lawrence did not by any means lose at this point his impressionistic power. But already in *The Rainbow* it is directed more closely to the realisation of mental states and in the volume of travel sketches *Twilight in Italy*, published in the following year, the most impressive pages are of this order. Mr. Lawrence now begins to make the reader vividly aware of his struggle to get out of the pit, which body and soul have made between them, or at least to understand why he is in it. There is a hint of this in the remarkable first sketch, *The Crucifix* :—

"The body bent forward towards the earth, closing round on itself ; the arms clasped full of hay, clasped round the hay that presses soft and close to the breast and the body, that pricks heat into the arms and the skin of the breast, and fills the lungs with the sleepy scent of dried herbs : the rain that falls heavily and wets the shoulders, so that the shirt clings to the hot, firm skin and the rain comes with heavy, pleasant coldness on the active flesh, running in a trickle down towards the loins, secretly ; this is the peasant, this hot welter of physical sensation. And it is all intoxicating. It is intoxicating almost like a soporific, like a sensuous drug, to gather the burden to one's body in the rain, to stumble across the living grass to the shed, to relieve one's arms of the weight, to throw down the hay on to the heap, to feel light and free in the dry shed, then to return again into the chill, hard rain, to stoop again under the rain, and rise to return with the burden.

"It is this, this endless heat and rousedness of physical sensation which keeps the body full and potent, and flushes the mind with a blood heat, a blood sleep. And this sleep, this heat of physical experience, becomes at length a bondage, at last a crucifixion. It is the life and the fulfilment of the peasant, this flow of sensuous experience. But at last it drives him almost mad because he cannot escape."

Here already Mr. Lawrence is entering into the curious condition of torture which has produced his later books.

The earlier novels were comparatively normal. There is, in *The Trespasser*, a hint of that mysterious hatred between lover and beloved which puzzled Mr. Lawrence so much. But there is nothing very extraordinary in, for example, the keeper in *The White Peacock*, the man of "one idea : that all civilisation was the painted fungus of rottenness." There is nothing abnormal in the character of Paul Morel, in *Sons and Lovers*, the young man unbreakably bound to his mother, unable to give himself in love to either Miriam or Clara. In these books there is much that is good, normal, and in the ordinary tradition of the novel. Mr. Lawrence can create characters, although, because he is so little concerned with story or plot, one is apt to forget in which book each occurs. George Saxton might stray from *The White Peacock* into *The Rainbow* without producing any effect of oddness. Alice Gall, in *The White Peacock*, and Beatrice Wyld, in *Sons and Lovers*, are surely the same person : at any rate the mind very easily confuses them.

This at least must be said, however, that, though Mr. Lawrence's novels are often shapeless and straggling, they do produce an effect of real life lived by real persons. Even as late as *Aaron's Rod*, this power is distinctly noticeable. The opening scenes of that book, the Christmas Tree in Aaron's home, the bar-parlour at the Royal Oak, are paintings at once of extraordinary vividness and extraordinary solidity. Indeed, one might go through these books for a long time, picking out such things—the splendid last fifty pages of that disappointing work, *The Lost Girl*, which describe the life of the Midland girl Alvina with her peasant through the Calabrian winter, the death of Tom Brangwen, the rabbit-hunting in *The White Peacock*, and so on. These things stay longer in the memory than the complete books from which they come : they are at all events the body of Mr. Lawrence's work, if not its soul. And to them may be added here the more simple and successful of his two plays, *The Widowing of Mrs. Holroyd*, with its beautiful last scene, in which the mother and the wife lay out the body of the dead miner who has given them both so much pain.

I have questioned above whether the novel is the proper medium for Mr. Lawrence, whether, under other conditions than those of our day he would himself have chosen to use it. But he was at all events born in a time when, however tyrannically the novel was pointed out as his path, it was possible for him to get his verse at least taken seriously and not merely as a novelist's recreation. His first book of verse, *Love Poems and Others*, immediately followed *The Trespasser* ; and it contained many beautiful things. Verse, indeed, one was inclined to think then, was his proper medium : it seemed suitable for his impressionistic richness, for his intensity of concentration on the passionate and symbolic moment. There were poems here which equalled the grave and measured beauty of the funeral-scene I have already quoted :—

> " Into the yellow, evening glow
> Saunters a man from the farm below,
> Leans and looks in at the low-built shed
> Where hangs the swallow's marriage-bed.
>   The bird lies warm against the wall.
> She glances quick her startled eyes
> Towards him, then she turns away
> Her small head, making quick display
> Of red upon the throat. His terrors sway
>   Her out of the nest's warm, busy ball,
> Whose plaintive cry is heard as she flies
> In one blue stoop from out the skies
>   Into the evening's empty hall."

There were also the dialect poems, including the queerly realistic and poignant little story of the girl whose policeman lover had been seduced by the widow he lodged with. Mr. Lawrence has since published three more collections, which contain many good pieces ; but on the whole I doubt whether verse is a medium which serves him better than, or even as well as, prose. From the first there was an awkwardness in his versification, a breathless scrambling to get at the rhymes, which was characteristic enough but which he would have been better without and which, I fancy, he would have been glad to get rid of. It drove him to free verse ; and in free verse he tended to become bombastic, hysterical and false. At his best he can write such a piece as this :—

" Along the avenue of cypresses
All in their scarlet cloaks and surplices
Of linen go the chanting choristers,
The priests in gold and black, the villagers. . . .

" And all along the path to the cemetery
The round, dark heads of men crowd silently,
And black-scarved faces of women-folk wistfully
Watch at the banner of death, and the mystery.

" And at the foot of a grave a father stands
With sunken head, and forgotten, folded hands ;
And at the foot of a grave a mother kneels
With pale, shut face, nor either hears nor feels

" The coming of the chanting choristers
Between the avenue of cypresses,
The silence of the many villagers,
The candle-flames beside the surplices."

At his worst he writes :—

> " And if I never see her again ?
>
> I think, if they told me so
> I could convulse the heavens with my horror.
> I think I could alter the frame of things in my
> agony.
> I think I could break the System with my heart.
> I think, in my convulsion, the skies would break."

It won't do : it reminds one irresistibly, though painfully, of the man in one of Mr. Wells's books, who said : " If she is dead, I will r-r-rend the heavens like a garment ! "

These two extracts are taken from *Look! We Have Come Through!* the book in which, as it seems to me, Mr. Lawrence made a definite attempt to discover whether verse might not be made to serve his purpose instead of the prose novel. I have always thought that in this attempt he must have been influenced by the German poet, Richard Dehmel—not so much by the " Roman in Romanzen," called *Zwei Menschen*, as by the lyrics in *Aber die Liebe*, which obviously tell the same story, but less deliberately. This may or may not be so : I have no means of telling. At any rate, there is a decided resemblance in more than one point between the two writers. Both concentrate, sometimes with success, on the passionate and symbolic moment. Both take an equally mystical and sensual view of life, and, in particular, of love. Both are often betrayed by the turbulence of their emotions into mere violence of language which does anything but express their meaning.

Of the two extracts I have given, the first, for

all Mr. Lawrence may say of the unity of his book, is distinctly detachable. It is "the sort of poem modern poets write," an impression, an anthology piece, beautiful, and valuable for its beauty, but inevitably with something of its author left out of it. Mr. Lawrence can do this, and often does ; but when he attempts to get more of himself into his verse, as a rule he fails. *Look! We Have Come Through!* fails by reason of both violence and obscurity. The language is often, as in my second extract, too turgid and exaggerated to convey any impressive emotion. And the meaning of the passionate moments which the book successively describes, their relations with each other and their significance for the persons who experience them are never clear. The central idea of the work never emerges so clearly as in the "Argument" with which it begins ; and even the "Argument" helps the reader very little to fit the separate pieces together into one scheme. But this explanation is worth quoting :—

"After much struggling and loss in love and in the world of man, the protagonist throws in his lot with a woman who is already married. Together they go into another country, she perforce leaving her children behind. The conflict of love and hate goes on between the man and the woman, and between these two and the world around them, till it reaches some sort of conclusion, they transcend into some condition of blessedness."

Conflict of love and hate ! Some sort of conclusion ! Some condition of blessedness ! The first phrase has a meaning which is real enough when we look at Mr. Lawrence's latest books. In writing the other two, he seems to have deceived himself. His world is a world of struggle, in which love is very much like hate, in which indeed one connotes the other and in which both are equally bitter. But with this endless struggle he is endlessly concerned. In *The Rainbow*, Tom Brangwen makes a speech at Anna's wedding, in these terms :—

" There's very little else, on earth, but marriage. You can talk about making money or saving souls. You can save your own soul seven times over, and you may have a mint of money, but your soul goes gnawin', gnawin', gnawin', and it says there's something it must have. In heaven there is no marriage. But on earth there *is* marriage, else heaven drops out, and there's no bottom to it."

The gnawing of the soul, its declaration that there is something it must have—these are things which are very real and very terrible to Mr. Lawrence ; and his acute consciousness of them is really the force which fills his work with life. In most men this sense of longing is roused from time to time by " some one's death, a chorus-ending from Euripides," is recognised by them as unappeasable and set aside, suffered or enjoyed, as best it may be. But Mr. Lawrence will not admit that it is unappeasable ; and he is for ever trying to find the proper satisfaction for it. He has sought the solution in love and marriage ; but, though he finds these indispensable to man, the perfect solution is not there. Tom Brangwen is unsatisfied, Will Brangwen is unsatisfied, Ursula finds that Skrebensky cannot give her what she wants and sends him away. *Women in Love* ends with the tragedy of Gerald and Gudrun, and with Rupert and

Ursula not quite happy, he because marriage does not give him all he demands, she that he should feel this. Aaron Sisson finds that he cannot be the lover of the Marchesa del Torre because he " feels his wife somewhere inside him " : but he does not turn home to his wife. From marriage Mr. Lawrence turns to the ideal of comradeship which he finds in Whitman. In an essay on Whitman, he argues that we must not destroy marriage but surpass it and reach " the sheer friendship, the love between comrades, the manly love which alone can create a new era of life."

It would be absurd to attempt here to criticise the philosophical value of these ideas ; but it will be something if we can disentangle the effect produced by them, and by the passionate striving whence they spring, on Mr. Lawrence's work. They have beyond all doubt increased its wildness and unreality. The attempt to appease an unappeasable desire might be expected to transcend the ordinary means of expression ; and so here it has proved in several curious ways. It has led Mr. Lawrence's style towards a strange, almost childish naïveté. The author of *The White Peacock* knew all about literary English and accomplished prose. The author of *Aaron's Rod* prefers to write like this :—

" They were quite a little family and it seemed quite nice. . . . So Aaron went skipping off to his appointment, at seven o'clock. Judge of his chagrin, then . . . But need we say that Mr. Aaron felt very much out of it."

It is almost like a little girl telling a story in the nursery to her companions : it is not very remote from the style of Miss Daisy Ashford. Now is this the detestable deliberate naïveté of sophistication ? I think it is not. I think that Mr. Lawrence, under pressure of his desire to attain to some goal, has come to the single-mindedness of childhood.

So it is, I believe, with the distortions and unrealities of his later books. *The Lost Girl*, *Women in Love*, and *Aaron's Rod* are all, outwardly, ordinary realistic novels. The dress of the characters is described, their food is described, there are little satirical sketches of odd persons. But the principal characters are always and consistently abnormal both in their speech and in their actions. A novel, of course, which gave a pure reflection of normal existence would be a very dull affair. A novel must at least deal with an interesting case, must show its persons under some sort of strain : it must almost necessarily have in it some situation which is not usual. But a novel which is one long abnormality, which on almost every page diverges from daily experience, is a different business. And one remembers of what a tissue of events and conversations these novels of Mr. Lawrence's are made up. One remembers that amazing Italian touring troupe in *The Lost Girl*, the initiation ceremony by which Alvina is received into the Natcha-Kee-Tawaras, the wrestling match between Gerald Crich and Rupert Birkin, the tirade which Ursula delivers against Rupert. And one comes to the conclusion that these are not, and are not intended to be, human beings as we know them.

They are, in fact, the symbols by means of which Mr. Lawrence expresses what continually occupies his mind, the belief that somewhere there *must* exist some appeasement for the intolerable yearning which possesses the mind of man. Whether there is such an appeasement or not does not concern us here : it is enough if we have disentangled this as the chief motive force of his work. We have still to consider whether he is wise in presenting his symbols under the appearance of men and women from the coal-grimed Midlands. There are obvious disadvantages in this method. It is easy to say, as I have already said, that his world is peopled by ill-mannered, hypersensitive and hysterical lunatics. It is easy to exclaim that human beings do not speak like this, do not behave like this. It is a stronger complaint that from Aaron Sisson playing with his children and washing in the back-kitchen we are dragged with a sickening jerk to Aaron Sisson, an impossible mythological giant, making love in an impossible way to an impossible Marchesa del Torre.

Against this there is a good argument. Modern myths are difficult to invent and generally unwieldy when they are invented. We do not want Mr. Lawrence to take to classical machinery or to the concoction of Jurgens. Perhaps his clinging to the framework of ordinary life as the material for his books prevents him from flying off into the confused nightmares of Strindberg, who was often little more delirious than Mr. Lawrence can sometimes be. He is in no danger of forgetting that what he has to express, and the symbols he uses for expressing it exist, after all, only for the service of ordinary life. Above all—he is a man of genius ; and we must wait and see, without expressing any too dogmatic opinion, where the path he has chosen will take him.

We have seen already what the taking of this path has involved. He is the rare example of a man who, endowed with every gift for writing beautifully and movingly, has thrown them aside in order to follow the line of thought and feeling which his nature ordered him to follow. It is possible to say that the solutions he offers of the great problem oppressing him are empty and false. I think they are. I think there is no answer to this riddle. I think Mr. Lawrence would be a more prudent and a happier man if he were to abandon the hope of finding one. But then Keats would have been a more prudent and a happier man if he had not permitted himself to love Fanny Brawne. Much great literature comes out of passionate follies. Mr. Lawrence's passion may be a folly. He may be wrong in thinking that it is possible for us to climb out of the pit in which we lie. He may be wrong in looking at this life as a pit. But, if so, out of his error comes a flame of poetry, smoky, strange, and disconcerting as it may be, which is at least genuine and which is hardly paralleled by any of the novelists of his generation.

James Elroy Flecker

COMMENTATORS on literature have sometimes assured us that no poet ever dies too young, and that if any good poet's death is set down early he is allowed by some special dispensation to do the essentials of a whole lifetime's work in such few years as are given him. The theory has in it certain elements of comfort and the merit, for a theory, of not being demonstrably false. But if it ever presents itself at least to the intuitions as false it must do so when we consider the life and work of James Elroy Flecker. He died at Davos on January 3rd, 1915, in his thirty-first year, of an illness which had first shown itself over four years earlier ; and there is reason to think that when he died he was not at the height of his powers but at the beginning of them.

His short career was one not unfit for the training of a poet : he was, on the whole, lucky in it. "I think it worth while mentioning," he says, "that I was educated in one public school and have lived most of my life in another ; that I passed four years at Oxford and two at Cambridge, and that it has been my duty as civil servant to learn some eight or nine modern languages." This he says to prove that he speaks not ignorantly on education ; but it makes also by no means a bad grounding for the practice of literature. It was followed by some years in the Levantine Consular service, first as student-interpreter at Constantinople, then at Smyrna, then as Vice-Consul at Beyrout, with holidays in Corfu and Athens. The East to some extent moulded him and certainly gave him congenial material, though in the end he found he did not much like it. (He was decidedly a Philhellene.) But, says his friend, Mr. Frank Savery, he " liked his work as Consul, and he once said to me that he was very proud of having been a good businesslike official, thereby disposing, in his case at any rate, the time-honoured conception of the post as an unpractical dreamer." This may be put side by side with Ishak's enquiry in *Hassan* : " Since when had a bludgeoning policeman the practical good sense of a thought-breathing poet ? "

He was very proud to be a poet and unusually conscious of being one. He never used the word without a little flourish. Most men of his generation avoided so calling themselves : they said, with a gesture of deprecation, that they wrote verse. Flecker had no sympathy with this attitude. " Here," he says, in the preface to his one novel, " is a tale such as only a Poet can write for you, O appreciative and generous public." He knew he was a poet, and he knew very well that to say so was to make a claim far greater than that of the man who says he is a solicitor or a painter. It implies not only a profession but also genius in the exercise of that profession. But he thought perhaps that it was almost his duty to make this claim, since he believed it to be a just one and since the poets of his time, by excessive modesty, had lowered in public esteem the whole caste of poets. I remember a notice by him of some book in a University journal, in which, to explain the use of one of his own pieces as an illustration, he asked why the exponents of the Higher Drama should have a monopoly of self-advertisement.

I remember, too, that I once asked Rupert Brooke to tell me all that he knew of Flecker. He answered very readily and talked for an hour or more. But of all that he said then I can now recollect only two things. He described how Flecker came to visit him at Grantchester, poling a canoe up the river at night. There were lanterns in the bow and stern and Flecker, dressed in flannels, a tall, swarthy and rather sinister figure, erect in the canoe, wore a garland of red flowers on his head. The second recollection is more to my point. He was, said Brooke, for ever talking about his own poetry. However the conversation began, that was always how it ended. "We used," Brooke told me, "to argue for hours which of us wrote the better poems. But, you know," he added, with a touch of self-conscious and laughing naïveté, "I could always see that he really *did* think his were the better."

It would be hard to doubt that he did. From the very beginning he must have felt the calm self-confidence of a man who has done *something*, whatever the relative value of that thing may be. In his early days at Oxford, according to Mr. Savery, he was astonishingly and unconventionally prolific—for then "a sonnet a month was about the maximum output of the lights of Balliol." Flecker wrote in profusion and had a taste for such lax and easy styles (for the imitator) as those of Swinburne and Wilde. Such of his juvenilia as have been given to us display chiefly a remarkable command of hard, tight versification, as in the translations from Catullus which are more than admirable performances for a schoolboy of sixteen. There is nothing else until we come to the *Fragments of an Ode to Shelley*, the precise date of which is uncertain, with their powerful precision of language and visual imagery :—

> " We cannot drain
> The spacious Sea for his rich store
> Of coloured weeds that shine in vain
> Upon the wide inhuman floor,
> The lonely yard where drowned men lie
> And gaze through water to white sky."

Fluent and copious imitations of Wilde and Swinburne are not available to be put in evidence: we must take Mr. Savery's word for them. When Flecker first appears before the public he seems to be rather costive than copious. His first book, *The Bridge of Fire*, published in 1907, contained thirty-five poems. Three years later, in a volume called *Thirty-six Poems*, he reprinted twenty of these pieces, some of them very drastically revised. The next year this collection was reissued with six new poems. In 1913 he published *The Golden Journey to Samarkand* ; and in 1915, after his death, appeared the tiny volume, *The Old Ships*. Lastly, the *Collected Poems* of 1916 added, apart from the juvenilia, only one of which has any intrinsic value, a very few unprinted pieces. There are, including the juvenilia, exactly one hundred and nine poems by Flecker available for the public.

The history of that first book is characteristic and instructive. He made his public appearance as the servant of certain definite and recognisable influences. He was inclined to be a decadent, he had read Baudelaire with enthusiasm, and he was not exempt from the reasonless, but not therefore less real, melancholy of poetic youth. In those days he was capable of writing and also of printing :—

"Songs breathed to the tremulous ditties
Of broken and harsh violins,
Songs hinting the rose and the vine,
Half drowned in the roar of red cities,
And youthfully pleased at their sins,
These songs I adore : they are mine."

No one capable of writing the fifth line of this stanza could possibly have meant what Flecker says in the whole of it. But the next page of *The Bridge of Fire* begins with more convincing testimony :—

"Helen of Troy has sprung from Hell
To claim her ancient throne:
So we have bidden friends farewell
To follow her alone.

The Lady of the laurelled brow,
The Queen of pride and power,
Looks rather like a spirit now,
And rather like a flower."

When *Thirty-six Poems* appeared, the first of these pieces had vanished (and it remains unreprinted to this day) and in the second, along with other changes, the word "spirit" was altered to "phantom." But Flecker's habit of revision is not to be illustrated by this one small and unimportant example. His aim was at definiteness, at saying the last conceivable word on the subject he had chosen ; and, with this end in mind, he found no change too drastic to be contemplated. On one occasion he shortened an entire poem by one foot in each line. This seems, to me at any rate, to suggest an exaggeration of the value of brevity ; and I am by no means sure that the second version of the poem is superior to the first. There is a modern prejudice against adjectives, which can be overdone. In this case, when "the lazy ghosts" became merely "ghosts" they lost something of value. And when, after hearing the bird singing in Hell,—

> "And some one there stole forth a timid hand
> To draw a phantom brother to his side,"

the picture is, at least to my mind, more moving than when—

> "And some one there stole forth a hand
> To draw a brother to his side."

But Flecker could be even more drastic than this. He suppressed the first verse of a poem in two verses and inserted the second verse bodily in another poem. He took a sonnet, a very beautiful one, and made it into four eight-syllable quatrains.

But this passion in him for revision, and yet more revision, was due not to any poverty of material but to an acute sense of the value of material. His mind was full of projects, and his desk was full of fragments; but he could leave nothing alone till he felt that it was as nearly perfect as he could make it. So long as it was not, it did not satisfy him, it did not express his thought. When, in 1913, he felt called on to explain his theory of poetry, he found that all he could do was "to praise a very simple theory of poetry which has for me a unique attraction—that of the French 'Parnasse.'" This preface to *The Golden Journey*, stimulating and suggestive as it is, and characteristic, cannot be said to be very successful as the formulation of a particular theory. Flecker can uphold his own school only by pointing to the faults of all the others:—

"The real meaning of the term Parnassian may be best understood from considering what is definitely not Parnassian. To be didactic, like Wordsworth, to write dull poems of unwieldy length, to bury, like Tennyson or Browning, poetry of exquisite beauty in monstrous realms of vulgar, feeble or obscure versifying, to overlay fine work with gross and irrelevant egoism, like Victor Hugo, would be abhorrent, and rightly so, to members of this school."

To tell us that bad work is rightly abhorrent to a Parnassian is not to tell us very much. The Preface is more illuminating elsewhere when it reveals to us not the intellectual theory of the author but his *feeling* about his own work. "It is not the poet's business to save man's soul but to make it worth saving"—this is one of the profoundest things ever said about poetry. And the Preface ends :—

"To this volume, written with the single intention of creating beauty, now the Moslem East, now Greece and her islands has furnished a setting. Those who are for ever seeking for what they call profundity of inspiration are welcome to burrow in my verse and extract something, if they will, as barren as the few cheap copybook headings to which they once reduced the genius of Browning ; in the attitude to life expressed in these pages, in the Poet's appreciation of this transient world, the flowers and men and mountains that decorate it so superbly, they will probably find but little edification."

To create beauty, to appreciate the world—one need not be a Parnassian or adopt any special theory to believe that these are the true aims of all poetry. But the Parnassians, on their guard against formlessness, tended to limit the sorts of beauty which it was legitimate to create. They were repelled by the egoism and gush of the Romantics ; and they did seek to exclude their own personalities from their works. One remembers how Verlaine, reared as a Parnassian, was seriously perturbed about the personal tone of certain pieces in his first collection, *Poèmes Saturniens*. The essential of their theory, which Flecker might have brought out but did not, was that the beauty they created was to be in the display of the subject itself rather than in the poet's feeling about the subject. They did in consequence often fall into the " unemotional frigidity " of which Flecker says they have been accused and against which the Symbolists eventually revolted.

Flecker did not bring this out, probably because it was a formula he would not have wished to defend. He himself was never more than half a Parnassian, though his practice is more consistently Parnassian on the surface than that of any other English poet. This school was to him in a literal sense a school, but it would never have been natural for him to allow it to become his world. He had decided affinities with the Latin temperament which attaches more importance to finish and precision than our race of amateurs of genius ever will. There have been other writers of English verse as careful and exact as he, but none, I think, so passionately conscious of the necessity for care and exactitude. Nevertheless, he had in his genius a strong admixture of what Matthew Arnold called the Teutonic paste ; and much as he admired Hérédia, whom, with others, he invoked to the defence of his theory, he could never have expressed himself within Hérédia's narrow and splendid limits. One needs, I think, to quote only one line to make clear this element in his genius :—

> " So, far away (sweet words are 'far away'!) "

I don't put forward this line as an example of either versification or poetry. It is in fact a piece of facile sentiment ; and the poem which contains it, though it was written in 1908, was never published by Flecker. But the spirit of it is easily recognisable and is one incompatible with thoroughgoing Parnassianism.

His " theory " then was one which was valuable for his education. There were, too, other affinities between Flecker and the Parnassians. He, too, loved bright colours and solid things with hard edges ; and from these he mostly pleased to draw his images. His poetry, whatever else it may be, is a solid thing, brightly coloured, with hard edges. He learnt exactitude in some measure in the useful school of translation. A poet who has learnt to translate the thoughts and images of another faithfully and without awkwardness sets about writing down his own thoughts and images with more confidence and a higher standard of accuracy. Certainly his translations of Baudelaire are without awkwardness and have the resonance of the original :—

> " Here, grinning for his wage, stood Sganarelle,
> And here Don Luis pointed, bent and dim,
> To show the dead who lined the holes of Hell,
> This was that impious son who mocked at him."

And at all times, whatever further judgment may be passed on it, Flecker's poetry is solid, resonant and satisfying, simply because he has taken the trouble to find for it the most exact and the best-sounding words. The poem which provides the title for his first book exists, as Mr. Frank Savery has told us, simply for that purpose. He thought of the title first and wrote the poem afterwards. But in both versions, that first published in 1908 and that which appears in the *Collected Poems*, it is a triumph of verbal pageantry. The changes are from inexact to exact, from what is comparatively commonplace to the unexpected. Thus, describing the Gods, Flecker alters :—

> " Crowned with soft light, attired with shining stars "

to

> " Robed with faint seas and crowned with quiet stars."

The first is sonorous and magnificent; the second, without giving up these qualities, makes a more poignant impression. But neither version has really much human feeling. In both, the poet is putting up a display of his power over language. In the first, he is conquering and resplendent : in the second, he is much more subtle.

This Parnassian side of him is often very obvious; and it did draw on him from time to time the reproach of " unemotional frigidity." The first impression one has of his work is of enormous control, enormous care. This one may take as it pleases one, as the mood goes. His language and versification are always suitable to his purpose and therefore delightful in themselves, even in such fooling as :—

" Thrice blest whose parrot of his own accord
Invents new phrases to delight his Lord,
Who spurns the dull quotidian task and tries
Selected words that prove him good and wise.
Ah, once it was my privilege to know
A bird like this . . .
But that was long ago ! "

They are still delightful in themselves, even in such a piece as *Pavlova in London*, where the derivation is obvious and confessed. They are no less impressive in such a show-piece as *Taoping* :—

" Across the vast blue-shadow-sweeping plain
The gathered armies darken through the grain,
Swinging curved swords and dragon-sculptured spears,
Footmen, and tiger-hearted cavaliers.
Them Government (whose fragrance poets sing)
Hath bidden break the rebels of Taoping,
And fire and fell the monstrous fort of fools
Who dream that men may dare the deathless rules.
Such, grim example even now can show
Where high before the Van, in triple row,
First fiery blossom of rebellion's tree,
Twelve spear-stemmed heads are dripping silently."

This is fine ; but it is a merely decorative picture which we, and the poet, contemplate with just the same quality of interest which we give to the figures on a piece of pottery.

Many of Flecker's poems, admirable as they are, are no better than this, which is in the true and exclusive Parnassian tradition. But, as I have said, he was no more than half a Parnassian and was far too self-confident and far too ambitious to exclude from his work the beauty which arises from the play of the poet's feelings on his chosen subject. The words "subjective" and "objective" are, I have always felt convinced, words which no critic ought to use unless he is prepared to explain in full what he means by them; and I have neither space nor inclination to explain here in full what *I* mean by them. But an exception may be permitted; and I think that a mere juxtaposition will do much of the necessary work. Against *Taoping* I will not quote the famous *Old Ships* (perhaps the most nearly *perfect* thing that Flecker ever wrote) but his hardly less magical fragment :—

" And I have heard a voice of broken seas
And from the cliffs a cry.
Ah! still they learn, those cave-eared Cyclades,
The Triton's friendly or his fearful horn
And why the deep sea-bells but seldom chime,
And how those waves and with what spell-swept rhyme
In years of mourning, on a summer's morn
Whispering round his castle on the coast,
Lured young Achilles from his haunted sleep
And drave him out to dive beyond those deep,
Dim, purple windows of the empty swell,
His ivory body flitting like a ghost
Over the holes where flat blind fishes dwell,
All to embrace his mother throned in her shell."

It is not possible to analyse the extent to which the poet's own mind and feeling enter into this, the extent to which the words that make up the picture release something which is much more than merely pictorial. But in the difference resides the whole potentiality of Flecker's genius.

I have said that he was self-confident and ambitious. He certainly had too much of both qualities even to be satisfied with lyrical poems, however poignant or however perfect. He attempted longer works, most of which are largely or wholly in prose. But (one must surmise) he knew from the first that in prose he could never get either the intensity or the surface which he desired. He never taught himself to write common argumentative or narrative prose, as he taught himself to write verse : in this medium, except when he used it for the purposes of the theatre, he remained an amateur. His chief works in prose are *The Last Generation*, a fantastic tale, *The Grecians*, a dialogue on education, and *The King of Alsander*, a novel. Of these, the dialogue on education is chiefly interesting because it so soon ceases to be a dialogue. The last person introduced, a " merry-eyed young man, with long, light hair, high cheek-bones, and a vivid colouring," soon silences the others and winds up the discussion by reading a long memorandum on the subject which is being discussed. The description makes one think of Rupert Brooke ; but often, or so I think, must Flecker thus have ended the disputations into which he was drawn. His sketch of a Utopian public school is challenging and even fractious, and also entertaining and inviting. But Flecker's main interest was in poetry ; and here, as elsewhere, it is possible to discern in him a violent impatience with the desirability of proving what he knows to be true. He is really anxious to get on with the work of writing poetry ; and he affirms the existence of an æsthetic law with a brevity that is disappointing :—

"Hateful to me are those ignorant and thoughtless people who say that taste has no rules and that art cannot be taught: never did a more pernicious heresy flourish. . . . For such law exists: it is not a mere matter of individual taste whether Velasquez be a better artist than Marcus Stone or not; or Milton greater than Keble or Vaughan. Velasquez *is* a better artist than Mr. Stone. The law is a complicated law, of course, but to consider its principles will be helpful; and it is refreshing for those who are bewildered by the disagreement of æsthetic experts to note that the greater knowledge these experts have, the more striking is their agreement in matters of appreciation."

And that is all we are allowed to learn about "such law." For Flecker had a very concrete, not a metaphysical or critical mind. He knew what he knew, and said so violently; but explaining was a different matter.

Of his two romances, *The Last Generation* probably owes something to Mr. G. K. Chesterton and has such a *dénouement* as pleases youthful geniuses. *The King of Alsander* is more elaborate and very much laboured. Like everything he did it was again and again rewritten. The focus of sympathy even shifted, in the different drafts, from heroine to heroine. Norman Price, drawn by some sort of magic from his country grocer's shop into the affairs of the obscure kingdom of Alsander, has two loves. One is Peronella, a girl of lowly origin, the other is a Princess. In the story as eventually published,—

"'When will you marry me?' said Peronella, 'and will you take me to England? O, say you will take me to England, Norman, and when you drive me round in your carriage all the world will say, " That woman cannot be of our town ; she is the most beautiful woman that we have ever seen." '

" ' Darling,' said Norman, ' let me think of this moment, of nothing but this moment, and always of this moment,' and he kissed her again.

" But the sun shone no more on Peronella ! And her lover was not thinking only of the moment. He was thinking of his life. Her pretty words pierced him like little darts of ice, and all the comminations of the sages could not have frightened him more than the maiden's innocent speech."

So he transferred his affections to the Princess. But there was a draft in which Peronella was the triumphant heroine ; and it is excusable to think that Flecker, despairing of properly finishing his novel, bundled it together and sent it to the printer with all its imperfections on its head. It has many beautiful and amusing and sensible pages ; but, compared with his poetry, it is a failure.

His greatest work is also unfinished ; for I refuse to believe that Flecker, alive and in good health, would have been able to leave *Hassan* as we have it to-day. But there is something fitting in the fact that a poet who achieved perfection so soon, and so soon found that it hampered his ambitions, should have been obliged to leave this tremendous play in a condition of trembling incompletion. We know now that he began to write it as a three-act farce. We know also that brooding on a single sentence in the first draft brought to birth the story which made it a tragedy. *Hassan*, as we have it, is a piece of work fundamentally unbalanced but held in a position of equilibrium by the despairing and successful efforts of a great poet. Flecker left it substantially where it is before he had reached the age of thirty.

The play has recently been produced ; and its reception has filled all those who are in any way concerned about the future of the English theatre with ungovernable optimism. Year after year we have reviled the theatre-going public and sworn that it would not know a masterpiece when it saw one. But the assertion was merely theoretical, because we had no masterpiece with which to put it to the test. Here at last is a masterpiece, and the theatre-going public seems to like it. But, if we look at it in the light of the bulk of Flecker's other work, it is a rather uncharacteristic masterpiece.

For the drama is generally considered to be the most objective and impersonal of all the arts ; and this Parnassian has written one of the most personal and personally revealing of all dramas. There can hardly be any doubt that in the theatre Flecker would have found his proper fulfilment, the true means for the employment of all his gifts. For he was witty, feeling, picturesque and deep. In the theatre he need have cast nothing away, for in a variety of characters and situations he would have been able to use each of these qualities in turn. His earlier play, *Don Juan*, is not likely to be produced except by misguided fanatics. It may never be printed ; and it is possible to assert without misgivings that he himself would never have printed it.[1] The plot is absurd. Don Juan is, in some unexplained way, an English aristocrat. He is engaged to the daughter of the Prime Minister, Lord Framlingham. Lord Framlingham

[1] It has since been both printed and produced.

is forcing on a war with Germany, to avoid which Juan shoots him on the Embankment. A statue of the dead statesman is erected in Trafalgar Square ; and it is this statue which drags the hero away to Hell. Lord Framlingham, it may be observed, recites while he is dying the poem Flecker printed as *The Dying Patriot.*

This contains the sort of caprices which a high-spirited young author might invent for his own amusement and that of a circle of private friends. Flecker would hardly have offered it to the world, though those who survive him need not feel themselves bound by the same scruples. The piece contains fine passages and fine scenes. It contains also examples of the compression and brevity which mark the great dramatist, as when the valet in angry terror asks Don Juan, " What are you ? " and Don Juan replies with the haunting and terrible phrase, " A spirit, troubled about departure."

Hassan is not imperfect in this way. It is a coherent and reasonable stage-play. But enough of the circle has been drawn to enable us to surmise the rest and to regret that Flecker did not draw it. The tragedy of Hassan and the tragedy of Rafi and Pervaneh are too nearly equal in intensity : the poet has not got his values or his grouping quite right. He was moving from a play in which Hassan held the centre of the stage to one in which Rafi and Pervaneh held it. That the process was arrested midway was no more than an accident. When in the prose of a careful writer we find a split infinitive we do not turn from him in disgust : we say to ourselves that there has been some mischance and we make a mental correction to what he must have intended.

It is not so easy to do this with a drama as with

a sentence. It is well said that you must not show unfinished things to children or fools ; and before such a work we may well count ourselves at least children. We can only guess at the manner in which the poet would have solved his problem. But we may make our guesses in the certainty that he would have expressed still more clearly the personal emotion which underlies the play. Hassan and the Caliph are both artists engaged in making pictures, whether in imagination or in fact. But the Caliph deliberately introduces pain as an element in his composition and Hassan as emphatically rejects it. The tragedy of Hassan is the tragedy of the existence of cruelty and pain ; and the play is in essence Flecker's own passionate revolt against it.

There was in Flecker a strong strain at least of interest in cruelty. One is struck by the lines in *The Ballad of Iskander* :—

> " He drank his bowl of wine ; he kept
> The flute-girls dancing till they wept . . ."

But he admitted cruelty and pain as elements in composition so long as he still thought himself a purely decorative poet ; and when he melted, when the whole larger horizon, of the life that was never to be, opened before him all his nature rose in anguished protest. There are phrases and scenes in *Hassan* which might be used to support the theory that Flecker had something sadistic in him. But, to me at least, these suggest only the great tragic poet's willingness to face the facts, to face them all the more willingly because they are terrible facts and facts of his own nature. The conflict is resolved when Hassan cries : " It is only for the torture that I speak : it is only for the woman that I implore. Say but one word: the sun will set so soon," and when, having thus incurred the Caliph's anger and trembled before it, he mumbles: " I am not ashamed to be a confectioner, but I am ashamed to be a coward."

This is not the time to dwell for long on the minor beauties of the piece. Its setting gave Flecker an easy escape from the Elizabethan jargon which haunts and paralyses the English poetic drama. He was able to pass from farce to tragedy with extraordinary lightness because his Eastern convention prescribed the same vocabulary for them both, and a new one. His dialogue, even at its most florid, is supremely comprehensible and speakable; and, what would naturally go with that, his sense of stage-movements is acute and sure. *Hassan* is an imperfect work only to children and fools, and to those who love Flecker well enough to divine, however dimly, what he would have made of it if he had been allowed the time.

I have spoken of his melting-point, of the moment when he was no longer satisfied, consciously or unconsciously, to create merely external and material beauty. There was undoubtedly a change in him towards the end of his life, though one cannot name an exact date for the change. A poet does not make a New Year's Day resolution and write thereafter in a different manner. The new manner shows itself at first in a phrase or a line or perhaps even a whole poem which surprises its author. But " if it is of God it will grow " ; and with Flecker it grew.

As there is no date to be set down for the change, it does not matter that I have no precise information on the chronology of his poems. Indeed, I doubt whether this chronology could be presented in any intelligible form, for most of his pieces were kept so long under hand and went through so many versions that it is impossible to assign any one of them to any particular period. But certain of the poems in *The Golden Journey* and nearly all of those in *The Old Ship* stand definitely away from the rest of his work. He had schooled himself to a hard and definite technique, on account of which, as a Parnassian must, he sacrificed something. But all this was really only schooling, lovely things as it produced by the way. The time came when he freed himself from these self-imposed limitations. *Saadabad* makes, if one must choose, as good a point of departure as any :—

> " Broken fountains, phantom waters, nevermore to glide and gleam
> From the dragon-mouth in plaster sung of old by old Nedim,
> Beautiful and broken fountains, keep you still your Sultan's dream
> Or remember how his poet took a girl to Saadabad ? "

The general effect is of greater negligence, the colours are softer and perhaps richer, and the personal emotion is less restrained. The point is that a deeper note comes through the light notes of Flecker's inimitable versification. The culmination is certainly in his wonderful lyric *Stillness*:—

> " When the words rustle no more,
> And the last work's done,
> When the bolt lies deep in the door,
> And Fire, our Sun,
> Falls on the dark-laned meadows of the floor ;

When from the clock's last chime to the next chime
Silence beats his drum,
And Space with gaunt gray eyes and her brother Time
Wheeling and whispering come,
She with the mould of form and he with the loom of rhyme :

Then twittering out in the night my thought-birds flee,
I am emptied of all my dreams :
I only hear Earth turning, only see
Ether's long bankless streams,
And only know I should drown if you laid not your hand on me."

This poem is imperfect ; and probably, if Flecker had lived, he would have mended its tenth line. But, like the others of the same period, it shows that he had enlarged his scope just because he had gained sufficient control over his style to be able to do so without loss of exactitude. The change is so obvious that one is tempted to say that he renounced his old exterior brilliance. This would not be true ; but in these pieces the exterior brilliance appears to be dimmed by a new inner light. One turns to the piece placed last in the *Collected Poems*, which is called *The Old Warship Ablaze* :—

" They come at last, the bird-soft pattering feet !
Flame high, old ship ; the Fair throng up to greet
Thy splendid doom. See the long spirits, curled
Beside their dead, stand upright free of the world !

And seize the bright shapes loosed from blood-
warm sleep,
They, the true ghosts, whose eyes are fixed and
deep !
O ship, O fire, O fancy ! A swift roar
Has rent the brow of night. Thou nevermore
Shalt glide to channel port or Syrian town ;
Light ghosts have danced thee like a plummet
down,
And, swift as Fate through skies with storm
bestrewn,
Dips out ironical that ship New Moon.

Here there are certain negligences ; but they are allowed to pass by a poet who knows that what he has to say will make more effect in the rough state than if it is clipped and trimmed, and that a deep inner sense of style will carry him further than any surface brilliance and precision.

This is the point which Flecker reached before his early death. His place in English literature is a high one. He joins those whose careers we must think of as legends, however reasonably we may assess their substantive contributions to our poetry. But beyond the legend there *is* a substantial thing. The early poems are magnificent pieces of workmanship and in the later poems there is more than this. *Hassan* is a great play. And still the potential legend remains—of a vivid, eager, masterful and individual spirit, who devoted himself so passionately to his art that before he died it yielded itself to him and showed itself willing to express his inmost and most poignant thoughts.

The "New" Poetry, 1911-1925

It is now some fifteen years since the first faint beginnings of what at its height was called, without much elegance but not without a degree of accuracy, "the boom in poetry." The wave which then raised its head has run up the shingle and seems to have retreated again, at least for the time. The present, therefore, may be a suitable moment for inquiring whether it has gone back into the ocean to return in full flood, or whether it was only one of those waves which some accident of wind or current selects for a delusive prominence out of a falling tide.

That the movement, whatever it was, should have been described as a " boom " was not altogether the fault of the generation which produced it. Among the legacies which the Victorian age left to its successors there was one, in the sphere of literature, which has been an unqualified hindrance ever since. In that period literary creation and literary criticism began to develop a self-consciousness which they have not yet lost and show no signs of losing.

In previous ages the existence of great poets, no matter what interest or admiration they might arouse, was never the occasion of any twittering excitement ; they were, so to speak, the sort of thing which it was natural to have about. It might, indeed, be held at any given moment that there were none ; and that was an evil, an accident to be regretted, but not a thing to make any one despair of the race. It was like childlessness in a family ; and in the same way the appearance of a poet caused the warm but unastonished gladness which in healthy times is caused by the birth of a child.

The vast and sudden material prosperity of the Victorian age produced a different point of view. It seemed necessary that among its glories there should be a poet great enough to be worthy of it, and, for the first time, the interested public looked for that poet with a lingering anxiety lest he should not be there to be found. He was in fact found and, by great good fortune, he bore a certain resemblance, freely recognised by himself, to the chief poet of the Augustan age of Rome. But already the idea was abroad that great poets were a kind of creatures that existed in earlier times, but were not to be looked for now. Disraeli, writing of Tennyson to Carlyle, clearly implied this view : to him it was not possible to think that his own time should provide the equal of—one supposes—Byron. And when Tennyson died there ensued a feverish search for his successor which was as injurious to both poetry and all standards of criticism as anything could be ; and the successor was not forthcoming. Morris and Swinburne were still alive and had been virtually enthroned ; but neither was young and there seemed to be no young man acceptable even as a candidate for greatness. Mr. Kipling, who alone inherited Tennyson's popular favour, fine poet though at his best he is, was not quite fitted for the position Then, after the brief, unsuccessful burst which we generally call " the Movement of the 'Nineties," poetry fell for nearly twenty years into a greater neglect and contempt than it has ever known in all the history of English literature.

It was not that there were not good poets to uphold the honour of the art. It could indeed be argued that there have been periods of greater barrenness. But with each of the poets of that time there was something that stood in the way of public recognition, and led the critics to champion their favourites a shade too eagerly and too consciously. There were Francis Thompson and Herbert Trench. But Trench, at any rate in his more easily assimilable poems, was getting a good gleaning from Arnold's fields, and Thompson, though there is more to be said of him, is not unfairly described as a splendid anachronism. Mr. Bridges, the spiritual heir of Thomas Campion, went on performing his chamber-music to a very small if delighted and intelligent audience. Among the poets of the 'Nineties there were two of importance—John Davidson and Mr. Yeats. But Davidson mixed up good and bad so inextricably that to this day no critic has seriously attempted the task of disentangling them, and Mr. Yeats, the one poet of the 'Nineties who in English carried that world-wide inspiration to the point of greatness, so firmly proclaimed himself to be essentially Irish that every one believed him.

And the reading public during these years turned away from almost everything written in verse in a manner quite unprecedented. The public, to be sure, was changed, though the influences which produced the change and its characteristics are too many and too complex for analysis here. But it was larger and lazier, and, by way of the novel, it was more and more deliberately being led into pastures easier for it than the concentration of verse. It was certainly not the same public as had made the fortunes of Byron and Moore, had been by no means unkind to Wordsworth, and might have been as kind to Keats, if he had lived a few years longer, as it later was to Tennyson. But these considerations do not modify the fact that, during this time, the writer who felt verse to be his natural mode of expression, seemed to himself and to others to have drifted into a backwater, to have engaged in an occupation that had ever less and less to do with life. It is a relevant fact that during these years the poet had in almost all cases to bear the cost of publishing his work. It is a relevant fact that in organs of criticism the smallest space was given to consideration of contemporary verse and, even so, in a patronising and pitying tone. There existed in short an atmosphere of slighting in attention in which poetry could not flourish or even maintain a healthy, if humble, existence.

The reaction which has since taken place is generally considered to have some connection with the war, and indeed the " boom " may be considered to have begun in 1915 with the presentation of Rupert Brooke to the popular imagination as a romantic figure. For many persons, in some queer way, his life and death did seem to rehabilitate poetry, to give it once again some sort of standing as a serious, not a trivial, human activity. He became the type of a war-poet, and just the sort of critic who had spent the previous August in complaining that the Great War had produced no Great Poetry was now ready to declare that this was the sort of Poetry he meant. True war-poetry, poetry springing from the war in both substance and spirit, was to come later, and, when it came, was very different from Brooke's sonnets, which were the expression of an ardent civilian preparing himself to be a soldier. There is all the difference in the world, in temper, as in material, between his

"Blow out, you bugles over the rich dead," and Wilfred Owen's :—

> "What passing-bells for these who die as cattle?
> Only the monstrous anger of the guns,
> Only the stuttering rifles' rapid rattle
> Can patter out their hasty orisons."

The first is the abstract poetry of anticipation, the second is poetry of concrete experience. To this point we shall have to return later. In the meanwhile it is clear that during the first twelve months of the war there came into existence a vague but none the less powerful emotional craving which found more satisfaction in both the reading and the writing of verse than in any other form of literature. We did not in those days know what we were at, neither what war was nor the real nature of our reactions to it, and in that confused, distressed time the intensity of poetry afforded a relief and a tonic to strained spirits. There grew and spread widely an atmosphere in which poetry could draw upon life.

But, like many other things which have had a similar fate, the poetic revival began before the war and was already in existence to be fostered by war conditions. Perhaps there is no recent period of which our minds retain a less distinct recollection, as to details at any rate, than the three years preceding August, 1914. We certainly have almost forgotten now that in 1913 moralists were complaining of the modern mania for dancing, of the unhealthy frequentation of night clubs, of the freedom of manners prevalent among the younger generation, and of the immodesty of women's dress. In the same way we have almost forgotten that critics were speaking of a revival in poetry some years before the war, and that by this they meant both that better poetry was being written and that the intelligent public was taking a more living interest in it. And for both these contentions they could cite adequate proofs. There was a movement and a stirring, people began to argue, and even to quarrel, about poetry as though it were really of some importance, and—what is always a significant sign—the charlatan began to lift an alert and interested head.

If a date is to be fixed for this change, the year 1911, I think, will do as well as or better than any other. It saw the publication of Mr. Masefield's *Everlasting Mercy* and of Brooke's first volume, and these—not, for the moment, to consider their merits—caused a quite surprising amount of serious discussion. In the next year came the first issue of Mr. Marsh's *Georgian Poetry*, published by Mr. Harold Monro at the Poetry Bookshop—itself another sign of the times. Mr. Marsh claimed that English poetry had recently taken on a new power, and in this faith he compiled his anthology which was a greater success than its promoters had expected.

To trace any particular movement in poetry to its ultimate sources in the life of the people is hard and doubtful enough when history has put all before the critic and he is far enough removed in time to see events in some sort of pattern. I shall not attempt to relate this movement to the undoubted intellectual and emotional quickenings of the years before the war otherwise than by saying that it was clearly one of them. There are, however, two poets of the *interregnum* not fully recognised before this time, who are often credited with having influenced the Georgian poets.

And yet I doubt whether Mr. Thomas Hardy or Mr. A. E. Housman exercised more than a superficial or incidental influence in those early days. They were, rather, premature Georgians themselves, like guns secretly established and waiting for the course of events to unmask them. Certainly until this time their importance was not properly realised. Mr. Hardy was obstinately supposed to be a veteran novelist, who had turned poet, as a man might take up a retiring post, and who deserved to be indulged in this relaxation of his later years. Mr. Housman's *Shropshire Lad* existed in such isolation and was surrounded by circumstances so peculiar that it was almost impossible to look on it as a significant part of the main stream of English poetry. But both Mr. Hardy and Mr. Housman, in their different ways, turned from the exhausted and etiolated Tennysonian manner and from that Swinburnian manner which was so fatally easy for any imitator to acquire and so impossible for any imitator to put to the smallest living use. Poetry goes down the hill when poets mechanically look at things as their predecessors have looked at them. The change that occurs as soon as they rub their eyes and see things for themselves is generally slight, or appears slight, when criticism attempts to describe it. But it implies a return to reality; and the novelty, whatever it may be, is priceless. Mr. Hardy and Mr. Housman achieved this return, and each contributed a new method of using language, Mr. Hardy *compelling* words to evoke such emotions as he chose, and Mr. Housman expressing lyrical feeling in a simple, epigrammatic, almost lapidary style.

Neither, however, has at any time been considered a revolutionary, and yet this epithet, odd as it may now seem to recall it, was freely applied to the Georgians of 1912, who attempted the same return with less success. The most prominent and characteristic of them were Brooke, Mr. Masefield, Mr. W. W. Gibson, and Mr. Lascelles Abercrombie. The first two were accused of wantonly introducing ugliness into poetry, which should be used only for the embodiment of beautiful images. Brooke referred with rather rhetorical gusto to the physical details of sea-sickness and to the more unpleasant physical signs of senile decay. Mr. Masefield made his country brooks run over rusty pots and pans, and dealt in the violence of prize-fights and murder committed by a navvy on his mistress. Mr. Gibson avowedly turned from his early, rather pallid decorations to the nobility of labour, the tragedy of poverty and views from slum-windows. Mr. Abercrombie, besides some essays in Masefieldian violence of action, was violent in thought and language : his muse was decidedly muscular, and his prosody sometimes suggested the lumpy biceps of the Strong Man at a fair. All four seemed to be of Synge's opinion that, before anything else can be achieved, our poetry must learn again to be brutal.

All four, of course, sought the return to fact more consciously and with fewer resources than Mr. Hardy and Mr. Housman. It was a rebellion deliberately undertaken against the exhausted conventions of the preceding twenty years, and only in a lesser degree, not wholly, a natural and instinctive new opening of the eyes ; and much of the rebellious violence was a sign of struggle and restlessness rather than of settled inclination. It must be observed too that the label "Georgian," though very happily chosen, had, to begin with, an exceedingly vague connotation. That first selection made by Mr. Marsh included several writers who were afterwards acknowledged to be incongruous bedfellows with the rest and with one another. But besides these there were poets who belonged to their time but can hardly be forced into the description which roughly covers the four I have already named. There was James Elroy Flecker, who avowed Mr. Housman as one of his masters in style, but who, aiming at the creation of concrete beauty, really felt stronger affinities with the French Parnassians. Mr. Harold Monro made odd excursions into a half-world of dreams, merging into nightmare, that had at moments a reality of its own. And there was the unassuming but very cunning naivety of Mr. W. H. Davies's small poems upon birds, bees, flowers, and children, which afterwards had a great deal to answer for. Also, there was Mr. de la Mare, expressing, by symbols of magic and by magically subtle rhythms, a very human attitude towards life. In all of them, in their degrees, was the element of novelty, the new opening of the eyes. In these four whom I have just mentioned it was perhaps more natural, there was less conscious rebellion, than in the others. But no formula, however ingenious, can impose the unity of a school on the first Georgians, who worked from different inspirations and in many cases were not personally known to one another.

Then came the war, and Brooke died in the French hospital-ship off Scyros, and Flecker in the sanitarium at Davos. These accidental happenings touched the imagination of a public which erroneously believed it to be characteristic of good poets to die young, and encouraged the growth of that new atmosphere of appreciation to which I have already referred. The emotions of war became a forcing-house for this very tender shoot of a poetic revival. It was inevitable that sentimentality should rage, and the early war-poetry was of a predominantly sentimental character. Speculations have often been attempted as to the manner in which Brooke would have developed if he had lived. It is possible that his poems were only the youthful efflorescence of a genius not destined for poetry at all, that he would have excelled as a critic, perhaps as a novelist, even more probably as a dramatist. What is as certain as anything can be is that if he had survived to accompany the Naval Division in its battles on the Somme in 1916 he would not have continued to write in the manner of the "1914" sonnets. These, fine as they are, are yet typical of all the work produced by the same crisis. A restless, dissatisfied, introspective generation, believing little in the possibility of war, and not at all that war could ever touch it closely, was suddenly, among infinite clamours and paroxysms of mixed emotions, summoned to prepare itself for battle. It was impossible that the poets of this generation should not be over-conscious of their own position, of their own emotions. The attitude of patriotism or of self-sacrifice into which the moment threw them was, for the moment, the sole reality. They knew that they had chosen to fight: the concrete meaning of that choice was as yet only to be imagined. It was later, when some of them had seen real warfare in the trenches, that a more solid and more actual war-poetry began to be written.

The change wrought by experience may be seen if we contrast one of Brooke's sonnets with a sonnet written later by Mr. Sassoon. Brooke, having made, like thousands of others, his heroic choice, can comprehend its meaning only in general terms. He cries :—

" If I should die think only this of me :
That there's some corner of a foreign field
That is for ever England. There shall be
In that rich earth a richer dust concealed ;
A dust whom England bore, shaped, made aware,
Gave, once, her flowers to love, her ways to roam,
A body of England's, breathing English air,
Washed by the rivers, blest by suns of home.

" And think, this heart, all evil shed away,
A pulse in the eternal mind, no less
Gives somewhere back the thoughts by England given ;
Her sights and sounds ; dreams happy as her day ;
And laughter, learnt of friends ; and gentleness,
In hearts at peace, under an English heaven."

It is a beautiful poem, it is sincerely passionate. For a contrast to it I have chosen, not one of Mr. Sassoon's vivid, sharply drawn scenes of trench-life, but a sonnet no less personal than this. He fought and suffered : he suffered as much in the persons of the others as in his own. He revolted against the war and in consequence he was withdrawn from it. Then he wrote :—

" I am banished from the patient men who fight.
They smote my heart to pity, built my pride.
Shoulder to aching shoulder, side by side,
They trudged away from life's broad wealds of light.

Their wrongs were mine ; and ever in my sight
They went arrayed in honour. But they died,—
Not one by one ; and mutinous I cried
To those who sent them out into the night.
The darkness tells how vainly I have striven
To free them from the pit where they must dwell.
In outcast gloom convulsed and jagged and riven
By grappling guns. Love drove me to rebel.
Love drives me back to grope with them through
hell ;
And in their tortured eyes I stand forgiven."

The difference, not merely in degree, but equally in kind, of self-consciousness is at once apparent. Brooke's subject is the impact made on his mind by the imagined possibility of death in certain circumstances. Mr. Sassoon is moved by something a great deal more definite. His emotion is more urgent and more poignant, and the experience contained in the poem is at once richer, more complex, and more directly expressed. Of this nature was the true war-poetry which began to be written when warfare had become for many a fact of daily life. It makes up most of the work of Wilfred Owen and Mr. Sassoon, some part of the work of Mr. Robert Graves and Mr. Edmund Blunden. Of these, Mr. Blunden, who still retains a passionately remembering interest in his experiences of war, seems the most likely to give us a full picture of the life of those days. Removal in time has not weakened his creative grasp of it, but more and more enables him to disentangle its essential spirit from passing accidents.

But it was not only in writing of war that the new poets developed. More sprang up behind the first line, four more times did collections of

Georgian Poetry appear, and presently all sorts of anthologies of contemporary verse were produced. Critics and public continued to supply at least an atmosphere of serious attention, though, not unnaturally, there were protests against the floods of little books of verse which this atmosphere encouraged and against the discovery by too enthusiastic reviewers of a great new poet twice or thrice in every publishing season. But before long more serious notes of dissatisfaction began to be heard, and certain critics, some of them entitled to be listened to, began to find grave faults in much of the work that had been so much applauded. On the one hand, it was not revolutionary, it made no innovation in technique or in diction or in subject-matter or in thought, but continued in the ways of the poetry that had gone before it. On the other hand, it was told, and by such learned and acute-minded critics as Mr. Middleton Murry and Mr. T. S. Eliot, not to congratulate itself on continuing the tradition of English poetry, since a poet who merely derives from his predecessors, and presents their thoughts and images worn and at second-hand, does nothing of the sort.

Now strictly technical innovation is not at this point of time very easy to accomplish without an altogether disabling degree of eccentricity. The most revolutionary change of recent years is that suggested by the Poet Laureate's experiments in quantitative verse—experiments which, however, seem likely to be more useful in sharpening the ears of poets using the customary metres than in furnishing a new instrument for English poetry.[1] *Vers libre*, of course, is no new thing, and the

[1] The "New Miltonic Syllabics," produced by Dr. Bridges since this was written, have in them far greater potentialities.

truth about most *vers libre* was expressed by Mr. Chesterton when he said that it was no more a revolution in poetry than sleeping in a ditch was a revolution in architecture. There are exceptions. Serious attempts have been made in England during the last fifteen years to establish a technique of free verse, attempts largely inspired by the example of such French poets as M. Georges Duhamel and M. Charles Vildrac, who themselves were chiefly concerned to make a system out of the example of Walt Whitman. These attempts proved, it seems, that in free verse it is possible to achieve new effects without sacrificing the discipline, the precision, and the sensuous beauty afforded by regular metres, but that this is done only rarely and with great difficulty and that on the whole the few successes barely justify the many failures. Of all the earnest experimenters who at one time called themselves " Imagistes," only one has had anything like a consistent success, the American writer who signs her poems " H. D.," and whose beautiful but minute and remote talent is to be seen in such passages as :—

> " In my garden
> the winds have beaten
> the ripe lilies;
> in my garden, the salt
> has wilted the first flakes
> of young narcissus,
> and the lesser hyacinth,
> and the salt has crept
> under the leaves of the white hyacinth."

The pauses made by the short lines create a subdued, tenderly pulsing rhythm, and the form justifies itself. But is this anything more than a surer, because a somewhat drier and quieter, accomplishment of what Arnold attempted in *The Strayed Reveller*? It is to be noted that "H. D." has recently showed a tendency towards the use of rhyme and even of fixed stanza forms. And, with less austere spirits, free verse, by reason of its want of discipline, generally tempts to garrulous commonplace or to pretentious rhetoric. Mr. D. H. Lawrence writes :—

"And if I never see her again?
I think, if they told me so,
I could convulse the heavens with my horror.
I think I could alter the frame of things in my agony.
I think I could alter the System with my heart.
I think in my convulsion the skies would break."

—which he might not have done, if he had had even only a metrical restraint imposed upon him. I do not mean that there is never any difference between free verse and chopped, violent prose or that it is impossible for free verse to express emotion at the temperature proper to poetry. I mean that this happens only with exceptional persons or on exceptional occasions, and that nothing has occurred to suggest that free verse contains in itself any revivifying principle. The way of movement seems to be in the execution of bold variations on the customary rhythms and perhaps in the use of such unbroken fields as the rhymeless lyric.

The critics who demand that modern poetry should render more fully and more richly the modern consciousness, and the world it lives in, stand on surer ground. The most able of the critics who have made this demand, Mr. T. S.

Eliot, is also the most formidable of the poets who have attempted to comply with it. He began under the inspiration of Jules Laforgue, as Hamlet or as Pierrot, laughing bitterly at life and then more bitterly at himself for paying life so extravagantly serious a compliment; and, like Laforgue, he managed to free himself very noticeably from the conventional use of poetic ornament and image, choosing unexpected similes as, of an evening, "Like a patient etherised upon a table." This manner is deliberately adopted and has a coldness that is often repellent. But it is not just to say of Mr. Eliot, as some have said, that his is a mechanically excellent intellect which has mistakenly strayed into poetry. He has at times a genuinely singing note and, if he had chosen to write in a conventional manner, might have produced work easily recognisable as beautiful. But his most ambitious work, *The Waste Land*, affords an almost exclusively intellectual pleasure, and that of two kinds. One enjoys the effort of following his thought and endeavouring to ascertain his meaning. There is also a pleasure comparable with that to be derived from a very superior acrostic or from one of those crossword puzzles which cannot be solved without an exhaustive knowledge of the Latin poets. Mr. Eliot makes in his poem I forget how many quotations from other more or less well-known poems and furnishes it with notes referring the reader to various treatises on anthropology and the like for a proper understanding of his symbolism. The style suggests that the author, an acute analyst of poetic styles, has here attempted something like an operation of synthesis. Having resolved Marlowe, Jonson, Dryden, and others into their elements, he has sought to reassemble some of these elements as constituents of a style of his own ; but synthetic products generally lack a vital something which is to be found in the works of nature. What is more important to observe is that this poem expresses a typical mood of disillusionment : the modern consciousness finds the world in which it lives a waste land. Now disillusionment may be a source of poetic emotion like another, but it is an infertile source and, in practice, the poetry which issues from it is thin and lacking in heat. As a matter of fact, the modern consciousness is ill represented by modern poetry, but perhaps most narrowly by the poetry of disillusionment. And, it must be remembered, this, being a source of emotion like another, may bring forth only sentimentality like another. Mr. Aldous Huxley has gone perilously near this lapse. But then Mr. Huxley seems to have deserted verse for prose, which is probably a natural development.

It remains only to notice the writers who have sought to revivify poetry by the deliberate adoption of a new set of similes and metaphors. Miss Edith Sitwell believes that the senses of " the modernist poet . . . have become broadened and cosmopolitanised ; they are no longer little islands, speaking only their own narrow language, living their sleepy life alone. When the speech of one sense is insufficient to convey his entire meaning, he uses the language of another." This enables Miss Sitwell to declare that—

> " Each dull, blunt, wooden stalactite
> Of rain creaks, hardened by the light,"

and even to justify in prose her use of these words. It introduces a novelty into poetic imagery : one can only regret that what would seem to be so important a revolution in human consciousness should have resulted in poems of so little importance. Miss Sitwell (with whom, less strikingly, her brothers, Mr. Osbert Sitwell and Mr. Sacheverell Sitwell) has done something mildly novel in purely impressionist notation, But the intellectual and emotional force of the whole family does not appear to be equal to anything more than the occasional production of rather lively and bizarre assemblies of words, which, however arrayed, do not mean anything in particular. These writers are at all points on a level with the writers of magazine lyrics. They disguise their status by being meaningless instead of maudlin, and for this they should be given as much credit as the achievement may seem to deserve.

So much for the revolutionaries or conscious modernists. To call all the rest traditionalists would be to beg too many questions and to impute a unity much greater than they themselves feel and greater than in fact exists. But there is a distinction, hard as it may be to apply in individual cases, between the poets who have deliberately sought modernism along the path of one theory or another, and those who have encountered it, if at all, as led by their own natures and experience. It is among these that we must look for an answer to the question whether the poetic revival has justified itself.

It has justified itself in the sense that it has added to the canon of our poetry an amount of new work not yet to be estimated but certainly perceptible. It has been, however, disappointing. Two of the older writers are established. Mr. Walter de la Mare, gradually augmenting the body of his lyrics, was suddenly seen to be a writer who, if he had attempted no organised work on a major scale, had nevertheless ended by completely expressing a certain conception of life and a full cycle of experience. His glimpse into paradise and the world of dreams, his fairies and his goblins, attain to unity as the magical embodiment of a philosophy. The poem which ends :—

> " When music sounds, all that I was I am
> Ere to this haunt of brooding dust I came ;
> And from Time's woods break into distant song
> The swift-winged hours, as I hasten along,"

is a beautiful thing by itself, but it means as much in its place in his whole work as does a detachable passage from one of Shakespeare's plays. The same thing, that he has produced a body of work, not an assemblage of separate pieces, may also be said of Mr. W. H. Davies. His nature is simpler, his experience less rich and less deep ; but all his poetry is one in expressing an innocently sensual appreciation of the delight of the world.

The case of the younger men is different, and though some of them early produced work of fine quality, nearly all of them seem to have delayed in redeeming that promise. By delaying they have incurred the just charge of being "anthology poets," in the sense that their best work is detachable and makes a deeper impression when found isolated in anthologies than when read in their own collections. They have refrained from larger works, and not one of them has yet made it plain that the growing bulk of his lyrics can be regarded as a whole. Mr. Robert Nichols, in his second, and first noticeable volume, *Ardours and Endurances*, had a naïve magnificence, an exuberant imagination and a power of vivid language. But though he has made a fine attempt at a prose play, he has flagged in the writing of verse. Mr. W. J. Turner, by combining a power of so approaching common things, as to make them seem newly strange, with a fascinating imagery of distant and imaginary lands, suggested that he might be evolving a universe of his own, as consistent and exciting as Mr. de la Mare's. But of his last two books, *Landscape of Cytherea* (he meant *Cythera*) is wilfully obscure and tangled, and *The Seven Days of the Sun* is a perverse, though witty, piece of petulant eccentricity.

These are only examples of disappointments that have occurred during the post-war years. Mr. Blunden, working away with quiet assurance at his two subjects, the war and the English countryside, is producing a body of poetry that never fails in accuracy or sincerity, though his method is a little narrow and inelastic. His motive is perhaps the chronicler's desire to preserve two things which are disappearing from human knowledge, and this is not the motive most prolific of poetry. Mr. Robert Graves, delving into a subsoil to which he believes psycho-analysis has shown him the way, may have discovered a principle of poetic being for himself. It may be that the revival flags because inspiration, too violently stimulated by all events since 1914, is for a little while in need of recuperation. It may be that public encouragement is suffering from fatigue similarly induced. It is possible, as some assert, that the wireless will rejuvenate poetry by restoring to it the direct vocal appeal which it has been gradually losing over a period of some two thousand years. But it is certain that at this moment English poetry is in a depressed and languid, though by no means hopeless, condition.

Rider Haggard and the Novel of Adventure

It seems at first sight a peculiar thing that prose fiction, in its present profusion, should be one of the latest births of literature. This, which appears to correspond to a deep-seated appetite in the human race, ought to have a longer, and more flourishing, and less often interrupted pedigree than in fact we can find for it. To-day, with the generality of persons, a book means a novel, and reading means the reading of novels. It is useless to say, as is sometimes said, that most of the novels which pour in spate through our circulating libraries and over the counters of our bookstalls have nothing to do with literature. This is to give the expression of an opinion—however well grounded that opinion may be—the deceptive guise of a statement of fact. Literature is the written word ; and the poorest serial story in the morning's picture paper, on sale (if you are in time) at any bookstall, is a literary phenomenon, not unfit for examination.

I do not mean to begin by comparing the romances of Sir Rider Haggard with these. Unless our modern devotion to prose fiction disappears with all the abruptness and thoroughness of its coming, some of his inventions will remain among the most prized possessions of our race. But these and his romances are equally products of a recent development in literature which requires a certain amount of analysis before its results can be properly understood.

All literature is ultimately the reduction of speech to writing ; and no narrower definition than this can ever be anything but misleading.

The lyric poem is the cry of emotion, the drama is the argument, whether passionate or intellectual, and the novel is the tale which men tell one another when they have leisure for such announcement. Now the novel was, broadly speaking, the last province of speech to be conquered by writing. It appeared spasmodically in the ancient world and in the medieval world. Petronius wrote a novel, and there were Achilles Tatius and Longus. There were the medieval and Renaissance writers, such as the compilers of the *Gesta Romanorum* and Boccaccio, who in fact did reduce popular word-of-mouth stories to writing. But prose fiction, the written descendant of the first anecdote told by Eve to Adam about some beast in the Garden, did not begin to take definite and unassailable shape until some two or three hundred years ago. It was essentially an art of the people, and the people could not write or read. It lived on in inn-parlours and market-places and round country hearths in the winter.

Then came printing, and then the growth of the art of reading, and then—perhaps a more compelling influence than any other, though all of these are so closely bound up together as to make it impossible to disentangle them—we had the Industrial Revolution and the growth of the great towns and that strange simultaneous limitation and expansion of human interests. The man of the fifteenth century lived in a very narrow world. He knew little enough of this earth and next to nothing of the universe outside it. His range of knowledge was restricted indeed ; but his range of experience was full so far as it went. Nothing stood between him and the direct contact of life ; and his appetite for experience was directly satisfied.

But with the growth of mechanical civilisation, a new element, the element of safety, came into ordinary existence. The man of the Middle Ages was no doubt a realist about adventures and desired above all things to be preserved from picturesque happenings. But the man of the nineteenth century, relatively immune from battle, murder and sudden death and such manifestations of the unexpected, felt unconsciously that instincts developed through many thousands of years were being starved. And simultaneously the printing-press and the art of reading gave him a new way of quieting these instincts. The novel offered such varieties of incident as too many lives had begun to lack ; and the novel of adventure began a new and vigorous life.

The last years of the nineteenth century, the years of compulsory education first making itself felt, the years when the popular magazine was born, produced several novelists, who cannot be ranked among the masters of literature, and who would never think of demanding such a rank, but who made impressions too deep and too genuine on the imagination of their time ever to be passed over as negligible. In almost all of these there was some quality of adventure. Sir Anthony Hope Hawkins, in *The Prisoner of Zenda* and *Rupert of Hentzau*, succeeded by virtue of plots at once very striking and very simple and by placing cloak-and-sword dramas, without lack of verisimilitude, in contemporary settings. Sir Arthur Conan Doyle gave his hero a genius which was consonant with the spirit of the age in so much as it was romantically scientific, and he took this hero into the hinterland of settled society, into the domain of crime. Sir Rider Haggard, another author very rightly knighted for his achievements, took for his province so much physical hinterland as the sudden growth of European civilisation had left in the world.

Sir Rider Haggard's many books comprise a number of varieties. He has written narratives of travel and works on agriculture and even a volume dignified with the terrifying description Cd. 2562, which is a *Report to H.M.'s Government on the Salvation Army Colonies in the United States, with Scheme of National Land Settlement*—which scheme, of course, has not been adopted. He has also written a number of novels of the sort that was conventional in the 'eighties and 'nineties. These have in them (I am referring in particular at the moment, I think, to *Colonel Quaritch, V.C.*) old, choleric, spendthrift squires with beautiful daughters, wealthy and bounding parvenus, bounding after the said daughters, wicked, scheming lawyers, who are not at heart so wicked as they seem but are driven to extremes by being blackmailed by obscure, rightful wives. Such works as these are outmoded, and one can hardly believe that anything written by a man who could write one of them should still have any life in it to-day.

But Sir Rider Haggard's work is still very much alive ; and I do not believe that the day can be foreseen when his best books will cease to have any interest. He helps the victims of modern civilisation to find the adventure and variety and unexpectedness which are denied to them in ordinary life. He is the great teller of yarns, a man in the true succession of Othello, and whole generations of Desdemonas, both male and female, have fallen in love with his gift. Even to-day, though it is long since he invented any plot or any character which was genuinely new, he can still move us with the old magic.

"Well, if you will have it, many years ago, when by comparison I was a young man, I camped one day well up among the slopes of the Drakensberg. I was going up Pretoria way with a load of trade goods which I hoped to dispose of amongst the natives beyond, and when I had done so to put in a month or so game-shooting towards the north. As it happened when we were in an open space of ground between two of the foothills of the Berg, we got caught in a most awful thunderstorm, one of the worst that I ever experienced. If I remember right, it was about mid-January, and you, my friend, know what Natal thunderstorms can be at that hot time of the year. It seemed to come upon us from two quarters of the sky, the fact being that it was a twin storm of which the component parts were travelling towards each other."

The story is told by Allan Quatermain, who proceeds to discover an unknown white race in the interior of Africa. This race has strange customs and is surrounded by strange phenomena. We have heard so much before and can tell, within certain limits, how the story will develop. Nevertheless this opening of a story published this year has something of the same charm that we found in the opening of *King Solomon's Mines* when we read it in boyhood, the real opening with which the adventure begins to unfold :—

" 'What was it that you heard about my brother's journey at Bamangwato ?' said Sir Henry, as I paused to fill my pipe before answering Captain Good.

" ' I heard this,' I answered, ' and I have never mentioned it to a soul till to-day. I heard that he was starting for Solomon's Mines.'

" ' Solomon's Mines ? ' ejaculated both my hearers at once. ' Where are they ? '

" ' I don't know,' I said ; ' I know where they are said to be. Once I saw the peaks of the mountains that border them, but there were a hundred and thirty miles of desert between me and them, and I am not aware that any white man ever got across it save one.' "

Now it is true that Sir Rider Haggard has played a great number of variations, not all of them so very various, on this theme. Allan Quatermain is not his only adventurer, but most of them have something of Allan in them ; and there is a strong family resemblance between the other characters and all the different episodes. It is further true that no book by this author is, in a strict sense, well written. The English is of a rough and ready quality : for the most part it serves to get the tale told and there is no more to be said of it.

Sir Rider would indeed hardly claim to be called a careful craftsman or an accomplished man of letters. He has always bustled through his work and shown for the refinements of literature something of the contempt and distrust which Allan felt for the refinements of society. Some thirty years ago he confided to an interviewer some details of his methods of work :—

" Mr. Haggard claims to create every character in his novels, and he considers six months a fair time to complete an important work. . . . He usually writes some three or four thousand words a day, sitting down at a great oaken writing table, with a liberal supply of foolscap paper, about half-past four, working on till dinner-time, and again resuming the thread of his story at night for an hour or two.

But the same authority says of *She* :—

" It was written in six weeks, and a fortnight out of that time was occupied largely in doing a friend's work—reporting cases in the Divorce Court for *The Times*. To write a novel in little more than four weeks is a truly remarkable undertaking, the brilliant result making it a still greater accomplishment. Mr. Haggard sat down to write it with a very slight idea of the plot, only with the great creative character in his mind—that of an immortal woman—a type. A story which a lady once wrote and told him—the story of a woman and a cave—helped him in writing *She*."

One's first impulse is to exclaim that one might have known it. *She* does bear every mark of hasty and unconsidered improvisation. It is rambling and diffuse, the author's conception of his heroine is long left vague, the writing is rough and poor. It may have been a feat to write it in a month, but one could wish that Sir Rider Haggard had seen fit to be less spectacular and to devote to so promising a theme not less than twelve times as long. Yet the book and the legend which so much excited the admiration of Andrew Lang did not do so without reason. It was indeed natural for Lang to suppose that he, whose scholarship and style were generally wasted for want of something to write about, might profitably join forces with this robust and fertile but untutored imagination. He was wrong, of course. *The World's Desire* combines the failings of both parties to it and is a book much inferior to *She*.

But what Lang saw in Sir Rider Haggard's work is really there. He is a natural teller of tales but hardly at all a man of letters. The faults of his work are the faults we naturally pardon in a narrative delivered in the course of conversation. At their best, his stories have the corresponding virtues of raciness and vividness. They repeat themselves. There is again and again the white adventurer who has some motive for seeking his fortune in unknown lands. There is the hidden race, guarding a treasure of one sort or another. There are the strange customs and religious beliefs of this race, which, generally, is divided against itself at the moment when the adventurers arrive, so that they can establish themselves by throwing their weight on the side of one party or the other. This pattern makes the essential framework of more stories than I could enumerate off-hand. There are other obvious faults. Many of Sir Rider Haggard's books exhibit, especially in their opening chapters, a curiously wandering diffuseness and lack of proportion, as though he had indeed sat down to write them "with a very slight idea of the plot." Take, for example, the opening of *Allan Quatermain*. Here we spend nearly a hundred pages over a story (by no means a bad one) of an attack made by the Masai on a missionary's house in East Africa. The savages capture little Flossie and hold her up to ransom, Allan and Umslopogaas devise a stratagem, there is a battle in which great slaughter is done by Sir Henry Curtis, there is a comic French cook, and so on and so forth. It is a good stirring little story, as such things go, but it has nothing whatever to do with the main theme of the book.

The reader permits his attention to be engaged by it, he follows it to its climax, and then it comes to a dead stop, and the missionary and his family disappear out of the book towards England, while Allan and his friends resume their expedition to Zu-Vendis. One can hardly resist the suspicion that the author, beginning with only a very vague plan in his head, was not at all sure that he would be able to make out his book to the requisite length and so snatched at any excuse for lingering by the way, as a man does who finds himself in danger of being too early for an appointment.

All these are the marks of the crude and mechanical novelist ; and, save when he is under the influence of certain inspirations, Sir Rider Haggard is no more than this. In the absence of these inspirations, he writes what seems an epitome of the deciduous leaves of the mercifully vanished three-volume novel :—

"Then at last Leonard broke out:

"'You do not speak the truth. I did not ask for your daughter's hand. I asked you for the promise of it when I should have shown myself worthy of her. But now there is an end of that. I will go as you bid me, but before I go I will tell you the truth. You wish to use Jane's beauty to catch this Jew with. Of her happiness you think nothing, provided only you can secure his money. She is not a strong character, and it is quite possible that you will succeed in your plot, but I tell you it will not prosper. You, who owe everything to our family, now when trouble has overtaken us, turn upon me and rob me of the only good that was left to me. By putting an end to a connection of which every one knew, you stamp me still deeper into the mire. So be it, but of this I am sure, that such conduct will meet with a due reward, and that a time will come when you will bitterly regret the way in which you have dealt with your daughter and treated me in my misfortunes. Good-bye.'

" And Leonard turned and left the room and the Rectory."

One's first involuntary hope is that some one had the humanity to offer the orator a glass of water with which to moisten his throat. But after this highly unpromising beginning, the story, which is *The People of the Mist*, becomes a characteristic and readable yarn. It follows the usual course—the preliminary adventure, this time with slave-traders, the hidden people and their superstition so easy to play on, the treasure, and the final escape. But this convention is Sir Rider's own and he contrives to vary the details very ingeniously ; and here the bridge of ice, passage across which is secured by riding on a tobogganing boulder, is a diverting and exciting novelty, just as Leonard's address to the cruel parents of his Jane is not.

Allan Quatermain was not very much at ease in civilisation ; and Allan, favourite child of his creator, is Sir Rider's imagination projected and re-embodied. It is thus that he comes to be so often used as a device for getting a story told. He appears in two different series, in those novels which deal with hidden races and in those which describe the wars of the Zulu nation and the fate of the House of Chaka. It is not too much to say that he extends himself beyond the limits of his own name and is discoverable under the skin of L. Horace Holly, from whose mouth issues the story of *She*. He made himself so convenient that the adventures accumulated round him have come to have an aspect of the absurd. One knew him tolerably well as an old South African hunter who "struck lucky" in Kukuanaland, and afterwards abandoned his wealthy ease in England for the final adventure with the white queens of Zu-Vendis. But who would have suspected, reading the story of his last exploit and his death, that he had had so many more adventures besides these and had left records of them all at home?

But, though this reflection may occur to one when one regards these adventures in the mass, yet each individual tale has its merits—varying a good deal, to be sure, from tale to tale. Allan is the ideal adventurer from the English point of view, for he has everything that is romantic except the pose of romance. There is indeed a great deal of Robinson Crusoe about him. He is, or represents himself to be, a shrewd, sober, practical man. He is never long out of battle and does terrible execution when he is in it, but he has no lust for combat. His thought when fighting approaches is to get it over as quickly, efficaciously, and safely as may be. He omits no occasion of telling us that the imminence of death made him tremble. But fear never unmans him: it only sharpens his wits. When he and Good and Sir Henry Curtis were threatened with death in the diamond-caves by the villainy of Gagool, it was he who thought to fill his pockets with precious stones before starting on the forlorn search for some means of escape. And he has heroic attributes. He is a marvellous shot—yet not an infallible shot, for that would take the flavour out of his exploits. In *Marie*, he is promised by Dingaan life and safety for himself and his companions if he can shoot on the wing three out of the first five vultures on the " hill called ' Hloma Amabutu,' a hill of stones where evildoers are slain." He carefully observes the habits of the vultures ; but he misses the first two, because, what he has not allowed for, they swerve from the flash of the rifle. After this he fires from behind them and triumphantly kills his three. He is also a great leader, crafty and resourceful. He is called " Macumazahn " or " Watcher by Night "; and I know not how often he has led to victory one faction or another of a hidden race he has come upon in his wanderings.

He bears a further resemblance to Robinson Crusoe, in that he never seems to be for long without a Man Friday of some sort. These faithful native servants vary a good deal. Umslopogaas, with his great and deadly axe, is himself an heroic figure and his body rests, after the last and finest of all his fights, at the top of the great staircase of the city of Milosis. The Hottentot Hans is different, combining loyalty unto death with more comic qualities, with a certain degree of knavery and a pronounced liking for the bottle. He is a grotesque and attractive rascal ; and one is sorry when he meets his death saving his master from the huge sacred elephant, Jana. But, it seems, there remained at least one further incident unrecorded in his past also ; and there may be more. With these I must not forget to include the unfortunate English servant of Holly and Leo Vincey, who died of horror at the awful transformation of " She." He has, I think, a touch of Sam Weller in him, and he too illustrates Sir Rider Haggard's avoidance of the unalleviated romantic pose.

To return to Allan Quatermain. He serves, I

think, as a symbol of that release of the imagination which converts a mediocre and unoriginal novelist into one who, whatever his defects, has characteristics of his own and has written several books with a distinct life of their own. This release takes him out of civilisation into the strange and unknown. Sometimes it is by an excursion into past history —though *Pearl Maiden* and *The Brethren* cannot be said to be among his most successful stories. *Cleopatra* and *Montezuma's Daughter* have more life in them, because they describe lost and mysterious civilisations which have a peculiar attraction for Sir Rider. His imagination plays a great deal round ancient Egypt (whither he has actually transported Allan Quatermain) and the relics of lost cultures in America and Africa fascinate him.

He is fascinated also by the extraordinary history of the Zulus. It is probable that this phenomenon of a warrior-race rising to greatness and falling to ruin within the space of a couple of generations is no new one in Africa. But in no other case has it been so fully known by white observers ; and it has particular features of its own. Sir Rider's series of Zulu books seems to me to be by far the finest part of his work ; and his story of the rise and fall of the house of Chaka, the Black One, attains at times an almost epic grandeur. For Sir Rider does give one the impression of having really got inside the minds of these people whom we too often regard as savages, and makes us understand the wild and cruel splendour of that brief military civilisation. The loves of Nada and Umslopogaas make a softer though tragic interlude in it. The death of Chaka at the hands of his brothers is an impressive scene of vengeance. Mameena, Child of Storm, the "Zulu Helen," is a heroine at once attractive and terrifying. And in these books more often than elsewhere does Sir Rider give sustained passages in which one's attention is not distracted from the feeling by a certain roughness and indefinable falling-short in the writing. Take the scene in which Mopo returns to the royal kraal to find that his wives and children have been killed and his huts destroyed and that he himself is under suspicion, from which he clears himself by undergoing torture by fire :—

"I rose, I praised the king with a loud voice, and I went from the *Intunkulu*, the house of the king. I walked slowly through the gates, but when I was without the gates the anguish that took me because of my burnt hand was more than I could bear. I ran to and fro groaning till I came to the hut of one whom I knew. There I found fat and, having plunged my hand in the fat, I wrapped it round with a skin and passed out again, for I could not stay still. I went to and fro, till at length I reached the spot where my huts had been. The outer fence of the huts still stood ; the fire had not caught it. I passed through the fence ; there within were the ashes of the burnt huts—they lay ankle-deep. I walked in among the ashes ; my feet struck upon things that were sharp. The moon was bright, and I looked ; they were the blackened bones of my wives and my children. I flung myself down in the ashes in bitterness of heart ; I covered myself over with the ashes of my kraal, and with the bones of my wives and children. Yes, my father, there I lay, and on me were the ashes, and among the ashes were the bones. Thus, then, did I lie for the last time in my kraal, and was sheltered from the frost of the night by the dust of those to whom I had given life. Such were the things that befell us in the days of Chaka, my father ; yes, not to me alone, but to many another also."

Two other themes have had on Sir Rider's imagination the same effect as the story of the Zulus. One is the version of theosophic doctrine which inspires that curiously simple and affecting little book, *The Mahatma and the Hare*. The other is his own legend of " a woman and a cave." *She* itself shows how the legend grew under his hand : the veiled and mysterious woman is taken more seriously at the end of it than at the beginning. I rather fancy that for some time Sir Rider played with the idea of extracting all the humour he could out of the situation of a barbaric queen in love with an embarrassed white man. But the legend proved too much for him ; and the last chapters lead on naturally to a sequel which has never, I think, been rated highly enough. The tone of *Ayesha* is more consistently on a high level than that of any other book outside the Zulu series ; and there is real beauty in the narrative of the pilgrimage through the snows of Central Asia with which it opens.

Here, too, there is abundancc of exciting incident. There is an excellent avalanche, and there is the plunge made by Holly and Leo over the precipice to apparently certain death in the river below. The mad Khan of Kaloon hunts his enemies with death-hounds ; and Ayesha is found dwelling in as impressive a natural wonder as is to be found anywhere in our author's work. This is, after all, the main texture and background of a fine row of romances. In general pattern Sir Rider has repeated himself again and again ; but in the matter of detail his invention is remarkably fresh and fertile. His adventurers seek escape through passages in the bowels of the earth, float down subterranean rivers, encounter horrific idols and assist at unheard-of religious ceremonies ; but these separate episodes do impress themselves separately on the mind and linger there. The comparison between Allan Quatermain and Robinson Crusoe leads one naturally on to say that Sir Rider has something of Defoe in him ; and there is this in the statement, that he gives reality to his romances by infusing them with an element of practical and matter-of-fact prose. The invention is fantastic ; but the author's real power lies in making solid the wildest of his fantasies. There is something characteristic in the way in which he continues to insist that " She " was really a woman of flesh and blood with like passions to other women ; and he actually makes the magic of Zikali more effective by recording all Allan's grumbling and doubtful materialistic explanations of it. It cannot be said that his imagination is unbridled ; but neither can it be said that he has no imagination.

The Centenary of Shelley

MR. SHAW argues in *The Complete Wagnerite* that if in the work of any artist he can discover a significant fable it does not matter at all whether the artist himself was ever aware that such an interpretation might be put upon his work. One may doubt whether the complicated fable of Capital and Labour which Mr. Shaw sees in the *Ring* is the best, or even a very fruitful, significance to find there ; but the rule in its general application is sound. Intention, it has been said, which in morals is everything, is nothing in art. It is nothing. The poem subsists in so many words written on paper. The poet may have meant by them this, that or the other ; precisely what, it is most unlikely that we shall ever know. But to us they mean something ; and what they mean to us is what is important for us. We may change the building that was raised for a barn into a tennis-court : we may use for a church what was put up to be a theatre. We may use or we may misuse : a whole generation may completely mistake the real capabilities of something which has been left to it. But the original purpose of the barn or the theatre is purely a question of archæology ; and, in literature, the more clearly we know archæology for what it is the better it will be for us.

For this reason the celebration of the centenaries of poets is not without its uses. The custom is no doubt very arbitrary. Granted that we ought to consider from time to time what, if anything, Shelley really means to us, one might expect the true occasion to arise not every hundred years but at intervals, say, of thirty-four, ninety-seven, and sixty-three years. But the important thing is that on such occasions we should be made to think, that matters of so much import should not be left to the winds of individual enthusiasm, that we should all think together and exchange our thoughts. The living fame of poets is a matter of corporate interest. The observances of the Church, as many of the irreligious have begun to discover, are not without their roots in the peculiarities of human nature. If the life of Saint Alexis exemplifies certain virtues of importance to the good life, then it is not a bad thing that those who wish to live the good life should be guided to think about Saint Alexis once a year. If Shelley's life and Shelley's poetry and Shelley's ideas have any meaning for us, it is not a bad thing that we should be guided to think about them once in a hundred years. The calendar of the Church is unassailable. The Positivist Calendar, with its heroes from Uruguay and wherever else, has its comic side ; but, with our modern custom of centenaries, we are beginning to form unconsciously, as did the early Church, a calendar of exemplary lives which may be of the greatest value to our civilisation. When we have to deal with an intangible thing, perhaps the more formal the occasion the better it is. A formal occasion has arrived for considering the present value of Shelley.

Shelley is still of importance to us. For some he is the figure of Arnold's much quoted quotation, "a beautiful *and ineffectual* angel, beating in the void his luminous wings in vain." Ineffectual perhaps; and yet, even so, even in this sentence, not without his effect on us. For some he is what, no doubt, Lord Eldon thought him, a young scoundrel; for others what his father thought him, a troublesome young fool. And I have heard a distinguished living poet declare his opinion that, out of all the human race, only Shelley may be named in the same breath with Christ.

In all these judgments it is clear that Shelley's character and actions are involved with his poetry; and there is something strangely appropriate in the fact that out of his life should have come the phrase "chatter about Harriet," which we commonly use to describe irrelevant gossip upon the private affairs of authors. It is the common phrase; but it is unfortunate, because we are all prepared to chatter about Harriet just so long as there is any hope of obtaining further light on some of the more mysterious episodes in Shelley's career. And why should we not? Who is ready to pretend that it is a matter of no interest to him? If we could get some reasonable understanding of why and how Shelley left Harriet for Mary, and what precisely was in his mind when he wrote to her from Troyes urging her to join them in Switzerland and adding some agreeable gossip about a mule and the fact that "Mary fears the fatigue of walking"—if we could find a reasonable explanation of this letter alone, we should have gone some way towards forming a clear image of an extraordinary being. To Harriet at least it must have seemed to come from a monster; and who can say how far the discovery that she had to deal with a monster, not a human being, may not have led her in the direction of suicide? But if Shelley appeared a monster in a particular relation, some strange combination of events and the elements of his character must have occurred to produce the appearance; and it would be worth the while of any student of character to discover what it was.

Shelley at all events was an extraordinary being. He seems even more extraordinary if we think of him, as we are usually bidden to do, as a sport in an old family of country squires. But his ancestry was not quite that. Sir Bysshe Shelley may have had a valid link with the Sussex Shelleys, whose lineage is irreproachable and impressive : indeed, the link is well enough established for ordinary purposes. But if there was no breach in the genealogy there was a sufficiently violent breach in environment and manner of life. Sir Bysshe himself was born in America, practised as a quack doctor, and had a peculiar talent for marrying heiresses. He achieved that feat twice ; and to his prowess it was due that his grandson was able to live an eccentric life without real financial embarrassment. We know very little about the early deeds of the great Sir Bysshe. I wish that we knew more, for one has a vague feeling that, *mutandis* very much *mutatis*, Percy Shelley took after his grandfather more than after his ox-like father, Sir Timothy, whose habit it was, whenever Percy did something more than usually outrageous, to rest secure in the approbation and support of the Duke of Norfolk. From quack doctor to poet is perhaps not so incredible a transition ; and one needs some early eccentricity in the family as a preparation for the author of *Laon and Cythna*. Sir Bysshe may in his youth have written verses of which he was afterwards ashamed. One has visions of a wild young scoundrel going from village to village in New England carrying his instrument-case as no more than a pretext. Perhaps Percy, if he had lived . . . but the vision stops there, pertinently reminding us that Shelley died a few weeks before his thirtieth birthday. We cannot indeed imagine what would have become of him ; but we ought to remember that he only just reached the age when most men begin to realise that their opinions have so far been purely experimental.

Perhaps Shelley would not have greatly modified his opinions. But, however that may be, we ought to be careful not to exaggerate their strangeness. He grew up in an age which saw the end of the Napoleonic Wars, the Congress of Vienna, the Holy Alliance, the Greek War of Liberation, and the beginnings of the Reform Movement in England—an age singularly like our own. Only a few weeks ago a political writer found that Shelley brought up to date made a good commentary on the year 1922, and, from the raw material of *The Mask of Anarchy*, produced the following stanza:—

> " I met Murder on the way—
> He had a mask like Poincaré—
> Very smooth he looked, yet grim ;
> Seventy journalists followed him."

Indeed it is probable that if Shelley's political views were lucidly and consistently set forth they would prove to be in the rear of those of most English Liberals. He was not a political fanatic. He could on occasion be almost numbingly moderate, as in the final paragraph of his *Proposal for Putting Reform to the Vote* :—

" With respect to Universal Suffrage, I confess I consider its adoption, in the present unprepared state of public knowledge and feeling, a measure fraught with peril. I think that none but those who register their names as paying a certain small sum in *direct taxes* ought at present to send members to Parliament. The consequences of the immediate extension of the elective franchise to every male adult, would be to place power in the hands of men who have been rendered brutal and torpid and ferocious by ages of slavery. It is to suppose that the qualities belonging to a demagogue are such as are sufficient to endow a legislator. . . . Nothing can less consist with reason, or afford smaller hopes of any beneficial issue, than the plan which should abolish the regal and the aristocratical branches of our constitution, before the public mind, through many gradations of improvement, shall have arrived at the maturity which can disregard these symbols of its childhood."

Nothing could be more reasonable. And if, in many poems, Shelley talked wildly of Tyrants and Anarchs, we must remember that he lived at a time when the Czar loomed huge over Europe, when the Bourbons were back in France, when the sinister voice of Metternich issued from the mouth of the Emperor of Austria, and when it seemed still uncertain whether the Sultan might not crush the aspirations of Greece. His opinions were not unnatural. His occasional vehemence can be easily explained. Only the moderation of such passages as that above quoted strikes the inquiring eye as curious. He was even conventional enough to take the revolt of the Parliament against Charles I. at its face value and without reservations. It may be doubted whether he had in any true sense a political mind, whether in any period less confused and anguished he would have troubled himself at all with the details of politics. But he was, nevertheless,—

> " A nerve o'er which do creep
> The else unfelt oppressions of this earth."

To a word in this we shall presently have to return. For the moment the point is that Shelley desired liberty and felt oppression most acutely in personal relations and in private affairs.

Here lay his greatest eccentricity. It was his religious opinions and his love-affairs that caused the greatest scandal to the public and the most annoyance to his connections. And even his religious opinions are not very startling at this point of time, as they were not unique in his own time. He held a sort of humanitarian Pantheism and he took over from the early Revolutionaries, with their doctrinaire hatred of kings, their equally doctrinaire hatred of priests. He admired Christ and detested the use which has been made of His name. He expressed his sentiments in an extremely violent way, but then violence of expression was natural in him, and the vehemence of youth had not had time to grow moderate before he died.

In his love-affairs he was endlessly and violently susceptible. It is a common human fault ; but Shelley is peculiar in that he elevated it into a sort of religion :—

> " I never was attached to that great sect,
> Whose doctrine is, that each one should select
> Out of the crowd a mistress or a friend,
> And all the rest, though fair or wise, commend
> To cold oblivion, though it is in the code
> Of modern morals, and the beaten road
> Which those poor slaves with weary footsteps
> tread,

Who travel to their home among the dead
By the broad highway of the world, and so
With one chained friend, perhaps a jealous foe,
The dreariest and the longest journey go."

And in this connection there is, I think, a discoverable significance in the letter to Harriet about Switzerland and Mary and the mule. It is the letter of a man who is acting on principle, or at all events has evolved a principle which completely covers his action. Perhaps the principle was not evolved, even unconsciously, to cover this particular action ; but one feels that Shelley arrived at it unconsciously, no doubt, to cover an ineradicable element in his own nature. Mr. Ingpen is one of many who have discussed his desertion of Harriet and what he says may be given as a sample of moderate opinion :—

" If Shelley had not thought her guilty, the fact that he was certain she no longer loved him was sufficient in his sight to make it impossible for him to live with Harriet as her husband. The convictions on the subject of marriage that he had expressed in *Queen Mab* in 1813 remained his convictions in 1814. He felt he was free to give his heart to Mary, with whom he was now deeply in love."

He did indeed. But hear Peacock's declaration:—

" He (Shelley) might well have said, after seeing Mary Wollstonecraft Godwin, '*Ut vidi! ut perii!*' Nothing that I ever read in tale or history could ever present a more striking image of a sudden violent, irresistible, uncontrollable passion, than that under which I found him labouring when, at his request, I went up from the country to call on him in London. Between his old feelings towards

Harriet, *from whom he was not then separated*, and his new passion for Mary, he showed in his looks, in his gestures, in his speech, the state of his mind, suffering, ' like a little kingdom, the nature of an insurrection.' "

Happy the man to whom strict principle points the easy way out of such a state ! And yet perhaps he was not entirely happy. It is easier for us than it could have been for his own world to realise his absolute sincerity. And a man who stoutly alleges principle as a reason for indulging his passions in a way hurtful to others raises round himself a barrier within which he can never, if he *is* sincere, be entirely at ease. He was perhaps at his most wretched in the Clare Clairmont affair. A discharged servant accused him of having made Clare his mistress ; and the Hoppners believed it and Byron believed it. There is no more unfortunate creature than a doctrinaire who is accused of an offence against conventional morals which he has not committed but which his principles would justify. One sympathises with Shelley's dismayed indignation—which is partly accounted for, of course, by certain alleged aggravations of the offence—but one sympathises also a little with Byron's credulity.

It is in his susceptibility to passion, or rather in his reasoned justification of it, that Shelley appears at his most abnormal. (I leave aside here the odd fascination which incest had for him, not because it is a disagreeable subject, for in him it is singularly deodorised, but because its origin and precise meaning are, and apparently must remain, quite mysterious.) He was by no means separated from his fellow-beings by any strong barrier in the other relations of life. His affairs were continually embarrassed, chiefly because of his generosity and the egregious spongers, Godwin at the head of them, by whom he was surrounded. But it is a mistake to think of him as being, like the legendary poet who hardly ever exists in reality, " up in the clouds," so far as the ordinary affairs of life were concerned. His business letters generally reveal the existence of distressing financial tangles, but they are always in themselves models of clearness and pertinence.

All this has to be said, though it has been said before and though it is not the whole truth. It is not the whole truth, because it minimises Shelley's extraordinariness and, when all is said and done, when all these reservations are allowed, extraordinariness remains our principal impression of him. But he was not out of the common because he hated kings and priests or because he deserted Harriet and was inflamed by Emilia Viviani, or because he wrote poetry, but by reason of something peculiar in his way of doing these things. You may laugh at Shelley when he distributes his writings on politics by putting them in bottles to be thrown into the sea ; you may execrate him when he leaves Harriet. But he acts consistently with himself and in a manner peculiar to himself. So it is with his poetry. It is consistent and peculiar, a thing which makes a definite impression on us, a defined field of study.

Like many works of art, it is most easily described by its general limitations. It is remote, unearthly, sometimes so rarefied as to appear positively arid. His second wife desired that he " should increase his popularity by adopting subjects that would more suit the popular taste than a poem conceived in the abstract and dreamy spirit of *The Witch of Atlas.*" "I believed" she says "that all (his) morbid feeling would vanish if the chord of sympathy between him and his countrymen were touched." And Shelley replied :—

> "For this one time
> Content thee with a visionary rhyme."

For this one time ! At the end of his career he was what he had been at the beginning ; and in *The Triumph of Life* there was no sign that the cloud-shapes of *Alastor* were beginning to condense into anything more solid and earthly. And when one considers the whole stretch of his poetry one is inclined to think of him as a "beautiful and ineffectual angel." How can anything so remote have any effect on us ? The sufferings of Prometheus are portrayed, the doctrine of love in *Epipsychidion* is preached, by a being not like ourselves, by a creature who moves in a different world and under different laws :—

> "The crawling glaciers pierce me with the spears
> Of their moon-freezing crystals, the bright chains
> Eat with their burning cold into my bones.
> Heaven's wingèd hound, polluting from thy lips
> His beak in poison not his own, tears up
> My heart and shapeless sights come wandering by,
> The ghastly people of the realm of dream
> Mocking me ; and the Earthquake-fiends are charged
> To wrench the rivets from my quivering wounds,
> When the rocks split and close again behind;
> While from their loud abysses howling throng
> The genii of the storm, urging the rage
> Of whirlwind, and afflict me with keen hail."

These are not to be described as inhuman symbols of human things : they are purely inhuman. And when in Shelley's poetry we come upon indubitable human beings in that Webster-like close of *The Cenci*, when Beatrice says :—

> " Here, mother, tie
> My girdle for me, and bind up this hair
> In any simple knot ; ay, that does well.
> And yours, I see, is coming down. How often
> Have we done this for one another ; now
> We shall not do it any more."

—when we read this we do not alter our opinion of Shelley's remoteness, we are merely astonished. What, we say, this visitant has studied us so closely ? he can speak our language so well ?

But Shelley, of course, *is* human, not really a visitant from another world ; and the peculiarities of his work may be at least partly explained on quite human grounds. The quality of his verse that most strikes one after its aloofness and inhumanity is its dizzy, confusing rapidity. He composes always at the pace which one expects only in a short lyric, even when he is writing an epic of some thousands of lines. His favourite images might repay inspection ; and of them all I think the most favoured are those which convey the idea of speed :—

> " At night the passion came
> Like the fierce fiend of a distempered dream
> And shook him from his rest and led him forth
> Into the darkness. As an eagle, grasped
> In folds of the green serpent, feels her breast
> Burn with the poison, and precipitates
> Through night and day, tempest, and calm, and
> cloud,

Frantic with dizzying anguish her blind flight
O'er the wide aery wilderness : thus driven
By the bright shadow of that lovely dream,
Beneath the cold glare of the desolate night,
Through tangled swamps and deep, precipitous
 dells,
Startling with careless step the moonlight snake,
He fled."

The impression made by this passage is repeated, not only in *Alastor*, but often through the whole body of Shelley's poems. No doubt the whole of Shelley's imagery, peculiar and strongly marked in character as it is, offers unusual inducements for psychological examination, but this particular image is perhaps the most obvious and will serve our turn :—

" And swift and swifter grew the vessel's motion,
So that a dizzy trance fell on my brain."

That is from *The Revolt of Islam.*

" We join the throng
Of the dance and the song ;
By the whirlwind of gladness borne along."

That is from *Prometheus Unbound.*

" The water flashed, like sunlight by the prow
 Of a noon-wandering meteor flung to Heaven;
The still air seemed as if its waves did flow
 In tempest down the mountains; loosely driven
The lady's radiant hair streamed to and fro :
 Beneath, the billows having vainly striven
Indignant and impetuous, roared to feel
The swift and steady motion of the keel."

That is from *The Witch of Atlas*. These instances, which I have chosen almost at random, might be many times multiplied. What they are intended to illustrate is the fact that, more often than not, when Shelley is in a state of high excitation he translates his feelings into images of intense and dizzying speed.

Now the statement that Shelley's poetry is the poetry of a neurasthenic means of itself nothing. That he was neurasthenic can, I think, be proved. There is no other way of explaining some of the facts of his life. It would explain his extravagant hypochondria, his conviction that he was born to die young, his unfounded dread of consumption and of such fantastic diseases as elephantiasis. It would explain the two curious incidents of the man who shot at him at Tremadoc and the Englishman who knocked him down in an Italian post office—incidents which he related with every appearance of belief but which his friends stoutly disbelieved. These things are convincing signs of highly disordered nerves; and it is impossible to avoid associating them with some of the characteristics of his poetry.

But we must take great care in establishing this association. Shelley's poetry is not interesting or uninteresting or valuable or worthless *because* he was neurasthenic. Only if we can discover a tangible cause capable of producing the impression which his poetry, considered in itself, actually does make on us, then the discovery is not without its importance. His poetry strikes us as removed, unearthly: it beats its luminous wings, if not in vain, certainly in a void. And its unearthliness is of a sort alone in English literature. Blake too is remote, but not in this way. He was a genuine mystic, so much absorbed in experiences for which language is not adequate that he never realised that the symbols by which he expressed them meant nothing to any one but himself. When Blake reported as literal fact that he had been in converse with an angel, he may have been suffering from an hallucination ; but it was an hallucination of a quite different order from that which persuaded Shelley that an assassin had fired at him through the window of his house at Tremadoc. There is nothing truly mystical in Shelley. His poetry springs from the world as he saw it, but he saw it as a man of exalted and super-sensitive nerves and mind. It is our world too, not, what Blake sought to give us as an alternative, the reality behind ; but it is our world distorted and made unfamiliar by the method of perception. Impressions crowded on Shelley with so great a speed and so much poignancy as to give him the sensation of dizziness which is so often rendered in his images. But he was, after all, a Pantheist, a nature-worshipper ; and such men are not necessarily, unless the terms be gravely misused, mystics.

It is worth noticing that the peculiarity on which I have dwelt reflects itself noticeably in Shelley's technique. This was not always at the height of perfection. One tends to forget his failures ; but they exist. The creator of the divine lightness of the *Epipsychidion* could write clumsy and lumbering verses, even after he had reached such maturity as he ever did reach :—

"My coursers are fed by the lightning,
    They drink of the whirlwind's stream,
And when the red moon is bright'ning
    They bathe in the fresh sunbeam ;
    They have strength for their swiftness, I deem.
Then ascend with me, daughter of Ocean.

I desire : and their speed makes night kindle ;
  I fear : they outstrip the typhoon ;
Ere the cloud piled on Atlas can dwindle
  We encircle the earth and the moon :
  We shall rest from long labours at noon :
Then ascend with me, daughter of Ocean."

He attempts (yet again) to describe speed, and he stumbles and hobbles. But the chief glory of his versification at its best is its extraordinary rapidity. I select for example a passage which does not describe speed :—

" Emily,
A ship is floating in the harbour now,
A wind is hovering o'er the mountain's brow ;
There is a path on the sea's azure floor,
No keel has ever ploughed that path before;
The halcyons brood around the foamless isles ;
The treacherous Ocean has forsworn its wiles ;
The merry mariners are bold and free:
Say, my heart's sister, wilt thou sail with me ?
Our bark is as an albatross, whose nest
Is a far Eden of the purple East ;
And we between her wings will sit, while Night,
And Day, and Storm, and Calm, pursue their flight,
Our ministers along the boundless Sea,
Treading each other's heels, unheedingly.
It is an isle under Ionian skies,
Beautiful as a wreck of Paradise,
And, for the harbours are not safe and good,
This land would have remained a solitude
But for some pastoral people native there,
Who from the Elysian, clear and golden air
Draw the last spirit of the age of gold,
Simple and spirited ; innocent and bold."

The fifth line of this excerpt cannot be called fortunate ; but the whole is simple, spirited, and bold, and, above all, rapid. Difficulties of syntax are as plainly avoided as hard collocations of consonants : it sweeps, like indeed the entire poem from which it is taken, in swift and easy motion from beginning to end. Towards this Shelley unconsciously worked ; and, in the lightness and speed of his verse at its best, he has no parallel in English poetry.

When it is so boldly stated, this attraction which he undoubtedly has for us seems to be no great thing. But the quality which I have sought to define as one of his limitations may also be attractive. I have heard it said : Byron for boys, Shelley for youths, Keats for men. The last term in the saying is pathetic ; but it at least recognises the fact that the seeds of a mature poetry are more obvious in Keats than in either of the others. Up to the end of a considerably longer life, Byron preserved something robustly juvenile, which it is improbable that he would ever have lost. If he had lived, he might have done anything, he would most likely have become a politician ; but, if so, he would have resembled Palmerston, who was called " Cupid," and was noted for the skill with which he dyed his whiskers. Keats was the only man born in England since Shakespeare who has given any promise of rivalling him. But when we think of Shelley we think also of something which not he but Keats wrote, in the preface to *Endymion*:—

" The imagination of a boy is healthy, and the mature imagination of a man is healthy ; but there is a space of life between, in which the soul is in a ferment, the character undecided, the way of life uncertain, the ambition thick-sighted : thence proceeds mawkishness, and all the thousand bitters which those men I speak of must necessarily taste in going over the following pages."

Hardly a word of this is directly applicable to Shelley. The ferment of his soul was strangely clear, his character was only too much decided, his ambition was clear-sighted enough. And yet this would make an excellent text for the sermon on him which in this essay I have endeavoured to preach. It is in the first place a declaration which could never have come from his lips. The seeds of maturity were not in him nor had he any consciousness that a maturity might come which would alter his attitude towards the world. And, though Keats attributes to his own period of adolescence certain qualities which we cannot justly identify in Shelley, yet Shelley's characteristics have a certain sympathy with those of youth always and everywhere. He was the perpetual adolescent. Adolescence is a time in which the nerves are at their highest tension, when the impact of new sensations turns life to dizziness ; and this is what is reflected in Shelley's poetry.

Shelley does correspond more or less to this period in the normal life ; and, because no period in the normal life ever vanishes without leaving a trace behind, he continues to mean something to everybody. He himself did indeed look forward to change and development in his genius. He says in the preface to *Prometheus Unbound* :—

"My purpose has hitherto been simply to familiarise the highly refined imagination of the more select classes of poetical readers with beautiful idealisms of moral excellence : aware that until the mind can love, and admire, and trust, and hope, and endure, reasoned principles of moral conduct are seeds cast upon the highways of life which the unconscious passenger tramples into dust, although they would bear the harvest of his happiness. Should I live to accomplish what I purpose, that is, produce a systematical history of what appear to me to be the genuine elements of human society, let not the advocates of injustice and superstition flatter themselves that I should take Æschylus rather than Plato as my model."

But in this, one feels, the conscious mind, rather than the unconscious speaks, while in Keats's very similar declaration one feels the opposite. Shelley is too precise in his programme : these works which are announced rarely appear. But Keats unconsciously offers evidence that he is rapidly passing from one state of mind into another ; and he lived just long enough to show that the evidence was not worthless. He might in time have written a work to be compared with *Hamlet* ; but Shelley would have written only a deeper and more nearly perfect *Alastor*.

There is a legend which relates that Keats wrote *Endymion* and Shelley *The Revolt of Islam* in a sort of competition—"a race over the Muse's meadows." Both poems must be called failures ; but one may dare the guess that of the two *Endymion* is the more widely read at the present day. Both have grave faults ; but the faults of *Endymion* are the faults of immaturity, while those of *The Revolt of Islam* are far more the faults of temperament. Keats's exuberance was a thing which time would curb. Shelley's enthusiasm was a thing which would stay by him as long as he lived. Both poems suffer from incoherence ; but Shelley's last great work, *The Triumph of Life*, even after allowance has been made for the fact that it was never finished, is much more incoherent than the pieces contained in Keats's last volume. It is, like all his works, a long poem written in the mood proper to a lyrical exclamation, and if you try the experiment of taking at random a number of passages from Shelley no one can decide on grounds of style whence they come—from drama or epics or lyrical pieces. They are all lyrical in spirit.

And, still, Shelley means something to everybody. Byron for boys, Shelley for youths, Keats for men : "The imagination of a boy is healthy, and the mature imagination of a man is healthy ; but there is a space of life between . . ." But there *is* a space of life between ; and that is precisely why Shelley, though he may beat his luminous wings in a void, does not beat them altogether in vain. He is the poet of adolescence : the poet of the age in which most of us receive our education at the universities, qualify as Parliamentary voters, form political opinions, fall in love, and even, sometimes, get married. It is a phase which passes, it is a phase much shorter than maturity, shorter perhaps than the strenuously untroubled age of boyhood ; but it is a phase which mankind is agreed to think of as having a memorable glamour as well as an anxious importance. Did the alchemists ever seek for the secret of perpetual manhood or of perpetual boyhood ? No : it was perpetual youth which they desired. The turmoils, the unreason, the happy and unhappy certitudes of that age, seemed to them at least acceptable. It is partly for this reason that so many have taken Shelley, whether for praise or for blame, as a type of the poet. So often, when we speak of poetry we are thinking, with an unconscious and an unfortunate limitation, only of lyrical poetry. And lyrical poetry is written best in youth, comes out of its turbulence and excitements naturally and impetuously like a geyser jet out of volcanic soil. One might almost say that Shelley's work is pure undifferentiated lyric. Its flow, its rapidity, its spontaneousness, its exaltation are almost more than anything it has to say or than any picture it shows us.

There is a sad moment in life when Shelley seems no longer to mean to us what he has meant. It is sadder, though perhaps less painful, if he has never meant anything at all. (There are also, of course, persons like himself who do enjoy a perpetual adolescence of the mind and who suffer no change in their feeling for him.) But that moment must be surmounted ; and after it he becomes a beautiful memory. But memories are things. Shelley survives and exists. If one has felt in tune with him at any time his poems continue to have a meaning ; and, so long as succeeding generations feel in tune with him, however often and however logically it may be pointed out that he is remote, unearthly, out of touch with life, he will continue to survive and exist.

The Return of Tennyson

MR. MAURICE BARING says of a certain poet: "He is safe in the Temple of Fame, which once you have entered you cannot leave. For this temple is like a wheel. It goes round and round, and sometimes some of its inmates are in the glare of the sun, and sometimes they are in the shade, but they are there ; and they never fall out." This is as good an image as has ever been invented to describe fluctuations in the fame of authors, but it is not quite complete. A man embarks on the roundabout in his lifetime, in the sun's full light, and sails away gaily into the shadows. He is forgotten or reviled or patronised. Presently he whirls back into the light and we are able to see that we ought not to have belittled him ; but we do not see him as his contemporaries saw him.

Perhaps this is progress ; and perhaps it is fair, as it is certainly comforting, to assume that in individual cases literary criticism does make real progress. Many minds pick over, sift, classify, describe the work of the master, and by this process make clear to themselves and others the precise nature of the sensations derived from his work. Up to a certain point, then, literary criticism may be regarded as making a closer approach to truth ; and when a man makes his second appearance in the sunshine we may expect to get a clearer notion of him than at the first.

The latest poet to swing prominently into view is Tennyson. Tennyson is at the moment in the air ; and it is a good thing. His reputation in his own day was inflated, though not, as we shall see, without good cause. Later there seemed a danger that he might be ranked, in practice, among the definitely lesser lights of English poetry, among the Brownes, the Drummonds, the Southeys, and the Moores. For some years little serious or new has been said about him, save an article by Mr. Squire and Mr. T. S. Eliot's casual but acute and reasonably just remark that "Tennyson, who might unquestionably have been a consummate master of minor forms, took to turning out large patterns on a machine." And now he is in the air. We of the literary world have our sudden little excitements and storm-centres, just as politicians begin all at once to talk of the Capital Levy or scientists of the structure and the disintegration of the atom. Tennyson is the latest storm-centre : at this moment any one who speaks of *Ulysses* may actually be referring to him and not to Mr. James Joyce.

This may be traced back, of course, to Mr. Lytton Strachey. Our generation has been accustomed to think of the Victorian age, under the influence of early teaching or sometimes in reaction from it, as an age of smug and stuffy virtues, of calm, unexcited and unexciting complacency. Mr. Strachey, not taking the Victorian age's view of itself, was not prepared to take this view either. He offered us instead a surprising and disconcerting vision, he showed us a sort of primeval forest inhabited by a fauna of prehistoric violence, sabre-toothed scientists, tusked and woolly theologians, statesmen with scales and wings and talons, and schoolmasters red in tooth and claw. A vision incredible at first, but soon found to be attractive ; and it was not long before it appeared probable that the chosen Laureate of so interesting an epoch might himself prove to be in reality more interesting than " school-miss Alfred." The studies of Tennyson recently published by Mr. Harold Nicolson and Mr. Hugh I'anson Fausset both obviously sprang from this discovery. We are now a stage advanced towards giving Tennyson his proper place.

In his old age he was a rough, grim, taciturn, forbidding figure. In his youth he was not the unexceptionable person that a reader of his sometimes namby-pamby verses might have thought him to be. He did not lead the life of Byron, nor yet of Verlaine, but Rogers said of him that he had such infirmities (presumably of character) as would for ever prevent him from supporting himself. What Rogers meant we cannot now guess. We do know that, as Mr. Nicolson rather cruelly says, " he drank just enough port to render himself hypochondriac ; he never drank enough port to forget that he was writing for an audience of young ladies." He was an uncouth, slovenly, rather intemperate and self-indulgent young man. He drifted and was idle, and selfish, keeping the unhappy Emily Sellwood on the rack of expectation for nearly twenty years. His was not an entirely amiable nor at all an exemplary character, but he did write most amiable and exemplary poetry for his audience of young ladies, who would have been most surprised to see him soaking port and making the air thick with tobacco smoke in some country tavern.

This uncouthness and these habits, which would have made him not altogether out of place as a character in *La Vie de Bohème*, developed into gruff overbearingness when he was old and eminent. In those days no one differed from him, except, once, Jowett, who regretted it. His household, and the guests who might be in it, deferred to him and he took their deference as of right ; there is something in his behaviour which subtly reminds one of stories of the monarch whose Laureate he was. He assumed a pontifical manner on all sorts of occasions. Mr. Nicolson quotes a remarkable paragraph from *The Times*, announcing (one presumes on the strength of an official communiqué from Farringford) that the Laureate had investigated the claims of a certain Captain So-and-So to be the originator of the Volunteer movement and was satisfied that they were correct. There were not wanting those who detected insincerity in his manner. Lady Butler, who was one of them, adds in her recent reminiscences a remarkable piece of observation. She thought she saw in the poet's eyes, when he was receiving adulation on an inferior poem, a glimmer of wonder and incredulity, as though for a moment the real soul peered above the screen it had made for itself.

But this arrogance of his later years corresponds to nothing that we know of his youth. There is no reason to suppose that when he went up to Cambridge he was convinced of the greatness of his poetic mission. That conviction was formed in the first place by his friends, the Apostles. Who has not known these undergraduate circles, whose members distribute among themselves the reversion of all the great places of the adult world ? It might not be modest in A. to put himself down for a future Lord Chancellor, but it would surely be wounding to the feelings of B. to cast him for anything lower in rank than an Archbishop. B. has much the same regard for the feelings of A. Among the Apostles, Hallam was to be Prime

Minister and Blakesley was to be Lord Chancellor. What could be more natural than that Tennyson, whose metrical abilities at least were obvious, should be marked down to be the great poet of the age? Oddly enough, the prophecy turned out to be accurate; but for this one which was fulfilled, there are many scores of such made every October term which are not. The Apostles, however, having entered him for this event, proceeded to train him for it.

Tennyson responded to the training and it moulded the rest of his life. But we need not on this account reproach the Apostles, for his character was such that the first strong influence under which he fell must have moulded him. He was plastic and impressionable and he had in him a strain of femininity abnormal even in a man of poetic genius: he had in him a greal deal of the yieldingness and submissiveness of his own heroines. His relations with Arthur Hallam prove this; and the famous reviewer of *In Memoriam*, who has been unjustly laughed at ever since, was not so far off the mark when he said that "these touching lines evidently come from the full heart of the widow of a military man." Other critics distinguished the same point, but, because they did so with less naivety and more reproach, are not so illuminating. The critic who said that "the taste is displeased when every expression of fondness is sighed out, and the only figure within our view is Amaryllis of the Chancery Bar"—the critic who said that insinuated unmanliness in Tennyson, and Tennyson was not unmanly. He was genuinely feminine. His attitude towards Hallam was quite extraordinary, and it is sufficiently indicated by an image he himself used to describe it:—

" He past ; a soul of nobler tone :
My spirit loved and loves him yet ;
Like some poor girl whose heart is set
On one whose rank exceeds her own.

He mixing with his proper sphere,
She finds the baseness of her lot,
Half jealous of she knows not what,
And envying all that meet him there."

This is precisely how the " village maiden " might have thought of the Lord of Burleigh ; and, in this context, the frequency of such situations in Tennyson's poems, which Mr. Nicolson has noted, is of peculiar interest. Hallam died ; and Tennyson was his widow, as *In Memoriam* testifies. But to call him unmanly on this account is to imply a perversion of spirit which is a grave error. Tennyson had merely in a quite unusual degree one predominantly feminine quality. When I say this I do not mean that all women love to subordinate themselves, to give devotion and to receive favour ; but this was the feminine strain in him.

It was abnormal, it singled him out from his fellows, and it was for him a plentiful source of weakness and indirection. May not the difficulties and contradictions which it involved have been the real cause of the melancholy which Mr. Nicolson rightly sees in him ? In that age and in that world, perhaps, a little more than in our own, it seemed natural and necessary for the woman to be guided and moulded by the man ; but, by that little, a man who desired to be guided and moulded was the more out of harmony with his surroundings. Tennyson's unhappiness, his unreasoned yearnings, were perhaps caused by his fundamental inability to take hold of life, and the disharmony must have been made more acute by the fact that in all physical characteristics and habits he was anything but feminine or effeminate. The woman in him was purely of the spirit.

But in the spirit that element worked very powerfully. It led him in the end to a position in which he could ignore life even if he could not conquer it. Mr. Nicolson has very acutely shown how he instinctively trimmed his sails to the winds of fashion of his time, how he responded to the spasmodics with *Maud* and to the "Fleshly School" with *Lucretius*. But these are extreme instances; his time was singularly unanimous as to what it required from a poet, and this was something neither spasmodic nor fleshly. What it wanted was respectable grandiosity, with a touch of domestic sweetness, and Tennyson was able to adapt himself to that demand without conscious effort. He may have been the slave of his age, but he wore his fetters as though they were garlands. He floated inevitably into a position which resolved most of his melancholy. He may not have been able to take hold of life, but it seemed as though life, after a certain time, capitulated to him voluntarily. During the "ten silent years" which followed the death of Arthur Hallam he was adrift and submerged, a sort of waterlogged wreck, and it seemed that anything might happen to him, for he was making no progress in the business of life. Then the natural adjustment of his talents to the requirements of the time brought him to a commanding position as easily as a cork comes to the surface of the water. It was as though a besieged city had surrendered out of some inadvertence to a besieger who had not in himself the will to summon it to yield.

When this happened Tennyson showed what would be called, in the modern jargon (which has its uses), an inferiority complex. His contemporaries, if they had recognised the symptoms, might have used more brutal language, and called him a Jack-in-Office. There is nothing in his relations with the friends of his youth, above all in his relations with Hallam, to justify the serene lordliness of his later years. Before he was established in a sacrosanct position he showed every symptom of weakness. He resented adverse criticism and sometimes flew into a passion against it, but when he had done so he apologised immediately with feminine effusiveness—witness his encounters with Christopher North and Bulwer Lytton. When he had become secure, not by strength of character but by sheer fitness for the times in which he lived, he growled down dissent. Now he not only could not, he positively would not, endure criticism. He imposed himself on a world which bowed down, not to him so much as to the ideal great poet which itself had designed and which he had executed.

There is now a natural tendency to underrate his importance in this capacity. Much of Tennyson which appealed to his contemporaries is to us, and probably to our posterity, of very little poetical interest ; but it is nevertheless of great historical interest. Our Tennyson to-day is a very different person from " the Laureate " of Queen Victoria. We are more than a little inclined to sneer at " the red fool-fury of the Seine " and " he thought to quell the stubborn hearts of oak." But these are undoubtedly good phrases, much as we are repelled by their meaning and tone. Is it nothing that

Tennyson should have had the ability to state even the prejudices of his time in perspicuous and lapidary verse? We know that there are reservations, poetical and historical, to be made about

> "A land of settled government,
> A land of just and old renown,
> Where Freedom slowly broadens down
> From precedent to precedent."

But this is what the Victorians believed about themselves and their country. It is true, perhaps, that you cannot write poetry about precedents, and that Tennyson and his contemporaries, when they imagined this kind of thing to be poetry, were, by our standards, deceiving themselves. But you can write remarkably good verse about precedents, as is here proved. Much of Tennyson's work is remarkably good verse, reflecting the current opinion of the times in which he lived. He was the spokesman of his age; and that is no inconsiderable thing to have been. To say that in this capacity he was no poet is quite beside the point: he was something. And, even in this capacity, he sometimes was a poet. I have no sympathy with the persons who do not think *The Charge of the Light Brigade* a good poem. I imagine that there can be but few who do not think the *Ode on the Death of the Duke of Wellington* a great poem.

When one has removed from his work so much of this element as may be necessary, a great deal remains, and still not all of it is on the highest level. I have quoted Mr. Eliot as saying that "he might have been a great master of minor forms." That, I think, is precisely what he was. He was evidently incapable of handling the major forms. His three most considerable works, *In Memoriam*,

Maud, and *The Idylls of the King*, are not homogeneous. Each is built up of small, more or less independent sections ; and they have consequently unevennesses and defects which are a totally different matter from the ordinary nodding of Homer. His plays, which could not be thus constructed, are, in spite of fine scenes and fine passages of verse, held by common consent to be failures.

But within his own range he moved at ease, and he had a sort of habit of perfection which is almost unique among the English poets. Modern critics often complain of the too striking felicity of his expressions. They are, in his own phrase, "jewels five words long, that on the stretched forefinger of all time sparkle for ever" ; and our taste to-day turns rather against the wearing of conspicuous rings. But I confess that I find it hard fully to understand why any one should resent his own delight on finding one of these jewels. They are of all sorts, these happy phrases, from "Bitter barmaid, waning fast" to "The wrinkled sea beneath him crawls." One remembers a dozen of them at once, and forbears to quote them. It is true enough that they sometimes stand out so much as to disturb momentarily one's enjoyment of the poem as a whole, and sometimes they are obviously dragged in from a notebook to provide an image of doubtful appropriateness. But even at the worst (and these worsts happen less often than is commonly alleged) they are poems in themselves, making precise and effective for us what before we have seen or felt only vaguely, and thus discharging in little the true function of poetry. More often they no more divert the attention than does a sudden beautiful cadence in a speaking voice. They do the contrary : they warm the mind with delight and quicken its æsthetic understanding of the poem.

And Tennyson's habit of perfection is clearly part of himself, not an affectation or a method deliberately adopted. If he had not had it, he would have been a different man, the spirit expressed in his poetry would have been different. No doubt it precluded the existence of other qualities in him. He could not, as I have already said, paint on a large canvas. It was not in him to press on to the great general effect, leaving the details to take care of themselves. For this reason his more ambitious works are built up of independent sections or they are failures. We do not think of *In Memoriam* as a single poem, because Tennyson could not so think of it ; it is a series of detached musings on the same theme. We do not think of *The Idylls of the King* as an epic because Tennyson did not conceive it, and could not have conceived it, as an epic : it is a series of short narratives in verse on related themes. And *Maud* is a collection of lyrics which decrease in interest and beauty whenever they attempt to " get on with the story."

But there were two things Tennyson, as poet, could do supremely well. He could write a lyric and he could tell a story in verse. He could tell his story, even when it was hardly worth telling in that medium. Much criticism has been directed against some of his lines. In *Enoch Arden* :—

" So past the strong, heroic soul away,
And when they buried him the little port
Had seldom seen a costlier funeral,"

is greatly disliked and so, in *Sea Dreams*, is—

" The glass with little Margaret's medicine in it."

For the first of these Tennyson had a defence. He said :—

> " The costly funeral is all that poor Annie could do for him after he was gone. This is entirely introduced for her sake, and, in my opinion, quite necessary to the perfection of the Poem and the simplicity of the narrative."

In my opinion both of these passages were quite necessary to the narratives in which they occur, and, therefore, to a certain extent condemn them as material, at least for the particular kind of verse which Tennyson employed. But in most of his blank verse idylls Tennyson tells his story with simplicity, with dignity, and with beauty. *The Idylls of the King* is not a great poem : the lines on which it was planned forbid that it should be. Here, too, the content is sometimes below the level of the workmanship. There are foolishnesses. The scene in which Merlin explains away Vivien's slanders against the Knights of the Round Table is bad enough anyway : it is not made any better by the incredible thinness of his explanations. But, taken one by one, these tales are of very high merit ; and, in their own sort, there is not much in English literature that surpasses them. There is no need here to speak of the *Morte d'Arthur*, but one recalls the extraordinary atmosphere of sick gloom suffused through the beginning of *The Last Tournament*, the clean economy of narrative in such pieces as *Gareth and Lynette*, the easy movement and vivid readableness of the verse in all of them. To the *Idylls* we must add those other narratives and quasi-narratives, such as *Lucretius*, *Ulysses*, *Œnone*, *The Dream of Fair Women*. These make one part of Tennyson's contribution to English poetry.

Of the lyrics the principal characteristic is that perfection which must lose something but makes what it does secure indubitably its own. There is no great force of passion behind them. If I am right in my opinion that Tennyson's melancholy and yearning spring from his inability to take hold of life, rather than from any mystical dissatisfaction with it, then we need not expect these qualities to connote any fervency of lyrical heat. And they do not. Tennyson is not a Catullus or a Heine. His was not a strong nature and no great struggle or trouble ever forced it into passion. But within the limits set by serenity and restraint he is one of the most successful lyricists in the English language. If there is no great intensity of feeling in his work, compensation is made in the shape of a sort of intensity of execution. The wine in his bottle may not be of the most potent but every drop of it is poured into the glass.

At the end of such a valuation as this, what has been said ? Little, save that Tennyson's best work gives the reader certain definite, unique, and valuable sensations and that his power of giving just these sensations and no others was something inherent in him, to be understood only by reference to the whole of his nature. The appreciation of poetry is a very imperfect faculty. We cannot help introducing into it factors which are ideally irrelevant ; and there, as elsewhere, more than half of what we see is seen only because we expect to see it. Therefore if we think of Tennyson either as a Great Victorian Figure or as a Great Victorian Bore, we are more than likely to go wrong with what he has written. Tennyson's new trip into the sunlight has been marked by a general and determined effort to find weaknesses in him ; and by some this has been resented. But with him the process is even more necessary than with most great men. The impression of him conveyed by the official memoir is like plaster over old oak and brickwork. It is smooth and unbroken, and it conceals the materials with which the house was built. When we strip it off, the surface below is irregular and broken ; but it is a real wall, and we are able to understand what holds up the roof.

Robert Browning

THE anticipatory Day of Judgment now being held upon the great Victorians resembles rather closely that once imagined by Mr. H. G. Wells, in which not the crimes but the shamefully comic weaknesses of mankind were to be the chief subject of inquiry. There is much to be said for this method of biographical revision. Tennyson was not, we feel, the impeccable compound of saint and hero which is reflected in the official life ; but it would not carry us much further if some devil's advocate were to attempt to represent him as a villain. Mr. Nicolson's discriminating and by no means unaffectionate humour is far more to the point.

But there is one Victorian figure which has not yet been subjected to this form of scrutiny and that, I think, because it is still something of a mystery. Robert Browning received indeed only in a restricted degree that canonisation which was so liberally bestowed on so many of his contemporaries. He was, by comparison, neglected in his early life. In his later years, his avowed admirers and propagandists were a rather solemn body of persons and the humours of their adoration did not escape the notice of the rest of the world.

Nor did the poet's own weaknesses go unobserved. With him, particularly in his last period, the contrast between the triviality of man and the greatness of his pretensions was always in evidence, in touches precisely to the taste of Mr. Lytton Strachey and Mr. Harold Nicolson. He was a great poet, writing great and largely incomprehensible poems.

While he was still alive, there was a Browning Society, studying *Sordello* and establishing little depots of explanation, in a manner reminiscent of preparations for a motor-trip across the Sahara. Meanwhile Robert Browning was periodically visible in London society, small, restless, vivacious, noted for his unfailingly immaculate lemon-yellow gloves, an indefatigable caller and diner-out, an immense talker at dinner-tables. Disraeli's one reference to him (though, of course, in matters of poetry, Disraeli, like Browning's father, was a man of the eighteenth century) is a somewhat irritable mention of having met somewhere " a talkative poet." A lady who saw him at a party inquired who was " that too exuberant financier." His exuberance and his talkativeness, something in his manner of dress, which was neither negligent nor elegant, but rather to be described as prosperous, gave rise to certain suspicions. He was said to be a Jew, which may be supported by the peculiar interest in the Jews shown in all his work, and by that oriental profusion and confusion of odd bits of remote learning, resembling, as Mr. Desmond MacCarthy once said, the rich jumble to be seen in the shop of an old-fashioned dealer in antiques. Some have even professed to trace in him symptoms of negro blood, which is supported only, if at all, by a family connection with the West Indies : there is certainly no evidence in his work of anything that could properly be called savage or primitive.

But the real mysteries do not lie here. One of them lies in Browning's youth, by which I mean the period before, at the age of thirty-four, he married Elizabeth Barrett and during which he wrote a considerable portion of his best work. Now, if the growth of poetic legend is in itself an important thing, if it is good for us to have before us living pictures of poets at the vivid, turbulent age when genius and character are being formed, then there is something to be said for poets dying young. When they live to be old, the events of their most active and formative years tend to grow obscured. The records made of them are made by persons who knew them as old men. They themselves, consciously or unconsciously, influence the spirit of these records in a way a young man could not. And, especially since the last century, the eventual biography takes a discreet and subdued form.

The result is that we know far less about the youth of Browning than we know about Keats or Shelley. We know, of course, many of the material and more or less indifferent events of his life. We know the conditions of his childhood, the famous story of his first introduction to the works of Shelley, and the circumstances in which he was dedicated to poetry. We know much about his travels, that he made a visit to St. Petersburg, about his friendships, his theatrical ambitions, his quarrel with Macready and so on. But what we know has a curious feeling of saplessness about it. One cannot help thinking that the author of those early poems the man who by his good looks, his charm and energy made so deep an impression on all who met him, on men so diverse as Thackeray and Carlyle, the hero of the amazing rescue of Elizabeth Barrett from her " darkened room," must have had a more varied life than any that is shown in the records, must have passed through some adventures before that one exploit of which we do know. No doubt this feeling is responsible for the story that he passed some of his youth wandering about with the gypsies ; but for this, so far as I am aware, there is no evidence whatever. Not long ago a volume was published which was to throw new light on his early years. Alas ! The new light consisted of an unconvincing argument that Browning was the real author of a well-known hymn, and a very improbable identification of the subject of *Pauline*. The mystery remains.

It is, of course, very largely of Browning's own making. Throughout his life he insisted, in a curious and rather suspicious manner, on the dramatic character of his work—" poetry always dramatic in principle, and so many utterances of so many imaginary persons, not mine." He is so anxious not to be misunderstood in this matter that he harps on it in the very titles of his books—*Dramatic Romances*, *Dramatic Lyrics*, *Men and Women*, *Dramatis Personæ*. He underlines it in *One Word More*, when he declares that for once he will speak in his own person :—

" Love, you saw me gather men and women,
Live or dead or fashioned by my fancy,
Enter each and all, and use their service,
Speak from every mouth—the speech, a poem.
Hardly shall I tell my joys and sorrows,
Hopes and fears, belief and disbelieving :
I am mine and yours—the rest be all men's,
Karshish, Cleon, Norbert and the fifty.
Let me speak this once in my true person,
Not as Lippo, Roland or Andrea,
Though the fruit of speech be just this sentence:
Pray you, look on these my men and women,
Take and keep my fifty poems finished ;
Where my heart lies, let my brain lie also !
Poor the speech ; be how I speak, for all things."

This was not indeed the only time he spoke explicitly with his own voice. Again he addressed his wife, after her death, in the closing lines of the first section of *The Ring and the Book* ; and he wrote an address to Edward Fitzgerald, which was certainly not "dramatic in principle." But he glanced at the poet's dissociation from the experience he describes in *How it Strikes a Contemporary*, and there is an almost defiant affirmation of his principle in *House*, with the famous—

> "'*With this same key*
> *Shakespeare unlocked his heart*,' once more !
> Did Shakespeare ? If so, the less Shakespeare
> he ! "

I do not wish to labour this point unduly, but I think that in it we may perhaps find a certain clue to the tangle (and it is a tangle) of Browning's poetry. I do not mean that we can discover, or indeed that there ever existed to discover, any Dark Lady of his youth, his relations with whom will make all his lyrics fall into a comprehensible scheme of self-revelation. We know all we need to know about the great love of his life and I think it is comparatively easy to trace its influence on his poetry.

Besides, the relation between a poet's experience and the form it takes in his poetry is always a variable and bewildering one, as can be seen from the well-meant attempts of innumerable critics to assume that Shakespeare, in his sonnets, set down, however obscurely, a number of biographical facts. Goethe was the most directly autobiographical poet who ever lived, and said that all his works were fragments of a great confession ; but we need a great deal of explanation, and evidence from contemporaries, before we can understand his poems on the factual plane. A poet may touch the skirts of an experience in life, but live it whole in his imagination. He may feel another man's experience so vividly as to make it his own. But all true poetry is, under whatever disguises, the record of something which has happened in his heart.

And to every poet there come moments when the setting down, for all the world to read, of this inner history seems a kind of shameful exhibitionism. It is then that he adopts disguises and symbols or, if he is lucky, like Shakespeare, finds at hand a healthy theatre in which he can speak his heart through the mouths of other persons.

Browning was not so lucky : the theatre of his day was no place for a man of genius, even if he had the true dramatic gift. It is certain that, for whatever reason, he was not successful in the writing of plays and rarely managed to present his characters in the round. And this, I think, increases the suspicion aroused by his so sedulous insistence on the dramatic (that is to say, non-personal) quality of all his work. There was a contradiction in him. Within his heart an immensely strong instinct of reticence was at war with his natural exuberance of self-expression. He feared always that he might too much expose himself to the gaze of the public and to this fear, I believe, eventually most of his obscurity and strangeness may be traced. The labyrinth of his poetry is a labyrinth he made so that he might hide himself in it.

Again—I do not intend to suggest that there was in his life anything which, from an ordinary point of view, it was at all necessary that he should hide. His reticence was like the shyness of persons, especially young persons, who cannot bring themselves to show enthusiasm or affection in the presence of others. Or, more fantastically, it might be compared to the belief of the savage that a knowledge of his true name will give his enemy power over him. It was simply an element, but always a powerful and often a determining element in his nature. On the one side was his reluctance to give any one a key that might unlock his heart, on the other the desire of that poet's heart for self-expression.

But, though he made the labyrinth to hide in, he did not quite succeed in hiding there. We are hardly likely, even by using this theory for purposes of the closest scrutiny, to find autobiographical details : he never spoke so plainly as his wife did in *Sonnets from the Portuguese*, which misleading title, by the way, he himself imposed. It is not, for example, really worth while to inquire who was the original of *Pauline*, for any youthful poet might have made that out of a trifle or out of nothing. But we can to a certain extent trace the working of his inhibition and we shall find, I think, that he is at his best when it is least effective. You follow him round the labyrinth and on the way you find many curious and amusing and ingenious things, put there to entertain and delay you ; but from time to time, if you press on, round a corner you will catch a full sight of the poet himself. We need not despise the " men and women, live or dead or fashioned by my fancy "; but Browning himself when we can catch him is the greatest and most moving of them all.

Distinctions of this sort must not be pressed

too far: it is enough if they seem to have a truth of a general sort. One might perhaps read something into the long suppression of *Pauline*, reprinted only in 1867 with a peculiarly anxious explanation of its non-personal character—"a sketch that, on revival, appears not altogether wide of some hint of the characteristic features of that particular *dramatis personæ* it would fain have reproduced." *Sordello*, however, is a clearer matter. The poem is a sort of parallel to *Alastor*, an account of the development of a poetic soul. But Shelley, though his fable is so remote and mythological, intends the direct expression of a personal experience and is not hard to understand. Browning declines from the crystalline air of mythology to the murk of history and involves himself in every complication of verbal obscurity and of local and temporal detail. Sordello is not himself a very interesting figure: he must depend to catch our attention on what of the poet has been put into him. Browning's first impulse was to put much of himself into Sordello; his second, a frantic impulse, was to conceal from every reader how much. The result is that baffling poem which numbs one in reading, so that by the time one reaches the end (if one ever does) one is too fatigued even to scratch below the repellent surface for a hidden meaning.

It is impossible to maintain that this work is anything but an artistic blunder. The charge is not that its subtleties demand concentration before the author's meaning can be obtained; it is that they frequently leave the profoundest concentration in doubt of it. And before Browning's declaration, some twenty years afterwards, that "the historical decoration was purposely of no more importance than a background requires," one is left agape. Let us take a passage at random :—

> " Tush ! No mad mixing with the rout
> Of haggard ribalds wandering about
> The hot torch-lit wine-scented island-house
> Where Friedrich holds his wickedest carouse,
> Parading,—to the gay Palermitans,
> Soft Messinese, dusk Saracenic clans
> Nuocera holds,—those tall, grave, dazzling Norse,
> High-cheeked, lank-haired, toothed whiter than the morse,
> Queens of the caves of jet stalactites,
> He sent his barks to fetch through icy seas,
> The blind night seas without a saving star,
> And here in snowy birdskin robes they are,
> Sordello !—here, mollitious alcoves gilt
> Superb as Byzant domes that devils built !
> —Ah, Byzant, there again ! no chance to go
> Ever like august, cheery Dandolo. . . ."

Several lines and phrases leap direct and vivid to the eyes, but what a " background " for " the incidents in the development of a soul " ! This is simply a turmoil of short and choppy waves like those one sees where two currents meet. The hydrographer can see meaning in that confusion, the psychologist perhaps in this ; but this, for the reader, is simply poetry in process of being strangled. It must be remembered that, three years before he wrote *Sordello*, Browning, in *Strafford*, dealt from full knowledge, with one of the less known episodes in the most intricate period of English history and wrote a drama which, whatever else may be said of it, is perfectly lucid. *Sordello* is not explicable save as the result of an acute mental conflict. Browning says in his exordium :—

> "Confess now, poets know the dragnet's trick,
> Catching the dead, if fate denies the quick."

Heaven knows what he has caught, but "fate" is an opposition in his own nature.

Few, if any, of his later poems rivalled the obscurity and confusion of *Sordello*. He found a way of yielding altogether to the inhibition without ceasing to write, a way which yet did not distinguish on the surface between those poems in which the inhibition ruled and those in which his true self emerged. His failure in the theatre closed one avenue to him, but he soon forced another and discovered in it the means to decided success. Poems like *Bishop Blougram's Apology* and *Andrea del Sarto* are not poems of the highest rank, are indeed only with difficulty to be reckoned as poems at all, but they are very interesting exhibitions of an acute and powerful intellect. Nor would it be reasonable, without further inquiry, to say that, if this be admitted, they should not have been written in verse. I will take a harder case than either of these. I will take that remarkable work, *Prince Hohenstiel-Schwangau, Saviour of Society*. Here is a passage from the beginning of it :—

> "First, how to make the matter plain, of course—
> What was the law by which I lived. Let's see :
> Ay, we must take one instant of my life
> Spent sitting by your side in this neat room :
> Watch well the way I use it, and don't laugh !
> Here's paper on the table, pen and ink :
> Give me the soiled bit, not the pretty rose !

See, having sat an hour, I'm rested now,
Therefore want work : and spy no better work
For eye and hand and mind that guides them both,
During this instant, than to draw my pen
From Blot One—thus—up, up to blot Two—
thus—
Which I at last reach, thus, and here's my line
Five inches long and tolerably straight :
Better to draw than leave undrawn, I think,
Fitter to do than let alone, I hold,
Though better, fitter, by but one degree.
Therefore it was that, rather than sit still
Simply, my right-hand drew it while my left
Pulled smooth and pinched my moustache to a
point."

Poetry, this ? No, for it lacks the ring and the temperature of poetry. An adequate interpretation of the real motives of that ill-fated Emperor of the French ? No—for perhaps he himself did not know what they were. But, even as the Prince says of his drawing, it is better done than left undone, and this for the world at large as well as for him who did it. It is a curious and discerning essay upon certain possibilities of the human mind. The verse does undoubtedly give lightness, speed, concision and something of an epigrammatic and gnomic touch to the development of the argument, and if we do, as we must, admit that the argument is in itself interesting, then we need not trouble to defend the work against the charge of being an artistic blunder.

Much of Browning's poetry does consist of such attempts as this at the purely dramatic, at the interpretation of other minds, at the rendering of experiences not his own. It was when he made these attempts that he deserved Wilde's witticism that "Meredith was a prose Browning—and so was Browning." He took refuge from himself in such studies and in what can only be called "reciter's pieces." He gave us extraordinarily interesting essays on the minds and souls of Mr. Sludge and Bishop Blougram, of Andrea del Sarto and Fra Lippo Lippi. On a lower plane are such poems of his earlier and later years as may be exemplified by *Incident of the French Camp* and *Pheidippides*. All these are fine works of literature, but they are not poetry in the sense in which Browning's best and most personal utterances are poetry.

I have said already that we know little of the intimate details of his life, but that of the most important of them all we know enough. Perhaps this too, if he could, he would have concealed from us. But his marriage with Elizabeth Barrett is a matter of history, sufficiently documented. It is a very remarkable incident. She was six years older than he, a confirmed invalid and in subjection to a ridiculously tyrannical father, and Browning's task was not merely to lend her something of his own strength but also to take on himself the responsibility of rescuing her from her life of invalidism. Is it fantastic to think that something of this is reflected in *The Ring and the Book*, in the story of the rescue of Pompilia from her brutal husband by Giuseppe Caponsacchi?

For this poem seems to me to represent the watershed of Browning's poetic life, being, but for a few lyrics, the date of which has been sometimes disputed, the last in which it is possible to detect the breath of personal passion. After this he developed the reasoned monologue, that curious study in psychology which approaches so closely to a later form of novel. He writes a score or so of spirited pieces, like *Pheidippides*, which stir the blood. But, until his very last years, we do not get again anything comparable to *The Lost Mistress* or *The Last Ride Together* or *Saul*.

It was perhaps unconsciously but certainly in consonance with his general principle of confusing what is in fact the main issue that Browning re-arranged the poems of his most vital period as they are to be found in his collected edition. *Men and Women* was, when it was first written, sufficiently homogeneous to have attached to it that beautiful dedication, *One Word More*, which I have already quoted. But later on Browning reduced it to thirteen poems, one of which is brought in from elsewhere. The rest, and all of them the most personal, are distributed between *Dramatic Lyrics* and *Dramatic Romances*.

These, under varying degrees of disguise, are the real Browning. There are descriptive passages where the dramatic mask is obviously unnecessary to shelter even the most sensitive soul, and there are also lyrics in which the strength of the emotion seems to disdain the protection of the mask. Apart from the confusion caused by Browning's redistribution of all the shorter pieces in his volumes published up to and including *Men and Women*, we have not often any definite information as to the dates of the individual poems. But we can take the three works, *Men and Women*, *Dramatis Personæ*, and *The Ring and the Book* as being the central mass of his poetry and also as being that part of it which was inspired by Elizabeth Barrett. Or, to put it in another way, we can describe it as being what he wrote while his feeling for Elizabeth

Barrett was sufficiently strong to overcome his peculiar instinct of reticence.

I have argued that before this, in that strangely mysterious young manhood of his, Browning must have had experiences all knowledge of which is denied to us. It is hard to believe, for example, that the author of *Pippa Passes* had kept himself so satisfactorily out of any kind of trouble as might be imagined by the reader of Mrs. Sutherland Orr's biography. There is much in this poem that is exaggerated and melodramatic, but there is also much that is as personal as an entry in a diary, and with the same stamp of vivid truth.

But it is in poems of a later date that this personal note is heard in full perfection, and when we hear it we hear the true Browning, no longer confined by an instinct of disguise, no longer obscure and involved, no longer grotesque, no longer intolerably learned. Everywhere, indeed, throughout his work any passage of description makes him simple and direct, sometimes to the damage of the dramatic convention he seeks to sustain. Pippa's opening soliloquy is a lovely poem which makes intermittent attempts, hardly more than perfunctory, to represent the peasant-girl who is supposed to speak. Take the first lines :—

" Day !
Faster and more fast,
O'er night's brim day boils at last,
Boils, pure gold, o'er the cloudling's brim
Where spurting and suppressed it lay,
For not a froth-flake touched the rim
Of yonder gap in the solid grey
Of the eastern cloud, an hour away ;

But forth one wavelet, then another, curled,
Till the whole sunrise, not to be suppressed,
Rose, reddened, and its seething breast
Flickered in bounds, grew gold, then overflowed
the world."

It is not Pippa, nor does it seriously purport to be : it is pure Browning, the Browning who wrote *Home-thoughts from Abroad* and that queerly living poem *Meeting at Night* :—

I

" The grey sea and the long, black land ;
And the yellow half-moon large and low ;
And the startled little waves that leap
In fiery ringlets from their sleep,
As I gain the cove with pushing prow,
And quench its speed i' the slushy sand.

II

Then a mile of warm, sea-scented beech ;
Three fields to cross till a farm appears ;
A tap at the pane, the quick sharp scratch
And blue spurt of a lighted match,
And a voice less loud, thro' its joys and fears,
Than two hearts beating each to each ! "

I have quoted this poem because it is a rather unfamiliar example of Browning's power of description. The last lines are perhaps the " dramatic " part of it, but it is not for them that the poem exists. The subject of the poem is the night over the edge of land by the sea. And this power is always exhibiting itself and, even when the poet is striving to be most impersonal, it reveals his person.

Sometimes it carries him away too far and intrudes itself : he does not always know how to place a picture in an emotional situation as so exquisitely he does in *The Lost Mistress* :—

> " All's over then : does truth sound bitter
> As one at first believes ?
> Hark, 'tis the sparrows' good-night twitter
> About your cottage eaves !
>
> And the leaf-buds on the vine are woolly,
> I noticed that, to-day ;
> One day more bursts them open fully
> —You know the red turns grey.
>
> To-morrow we meet the same then, dearest ? . . ."

Artistry can go no further than in the cunning, apparently careless arrangement of these lines.

And this is also, of course, one of the pieces which constitute the main problem of my present inquiry. It is a problem hardly to be resolved by any logical means : one can but make one's statements in seemingly dogmatic form and trust that they will suggest a certain way of looking at the poems. These pieces are not, so far as we know, founded directly on experiences in the world of fact, and they are not, therefore, in that sense, personal, may indeed be regarded, as Browning wished them to be regarded, as dramatic. But I submit that there is a real difference in spirit between *The Lost Mistress*, *The Last Ride Together*, *A Lover's Quarrel*, and some dozens more of the same order, and such pieces, obviously dramatic, as *Count Gismond*. Let us contrast a couple of passages first from *Count Gismond* :—

"This glads me most that I enjoyed
The heart of joy, with my content
In watching Gismond unalloyed
By any doubt of the event.
God took that on Him—I was bid
Watch Gismond for my part : I did."

This is from *The Last Ride Together* :—

"My mistress bent that brow of hers ;
Those deep dark eyes where pride demurs
When pity would be softening through,
Fixed me a breathing-while or two
With life or death in the balance : right !
The blood replenished me again ;
My last thought was at least not vain :
I and my mistress, side by side,
Shall be together, breathe and ride,
So, one day more am I deified.
Who knows but the world may end to-night ?

Hush ! if you saw some western cloud
All billowy-bosomed, over-bowed,
By many benedictions—sun's
And moon's and evening star's at once—
And so, you, looking and loving best,
Conscious grew, your passion drew
Cloud, sunset, moon-rise, star-shine too,
Down on you, near and yet more near,
Till flesh must fade for heaven was here !—
Thus leant she and lingered—joy and fear !
Thus lay she a moment on my breast."

It would be waste of space to argue that this is a better piece than that with which I have contrasted it, for it is one of the loveliest and most triumphant poems in our language. What I do contend is that it is in a different order of feeling from the other. It has the ring of personal feeling and, though the event may be imaginary, yet the poet has made the experience his own, as he has not in *Bishop Blougram's Apology* or *Andrea del Sarto*, and it cannot therefore be considered a dramatic poem in the sense in which these poems are dramatic. I suggest further that, even so, a shyness imposed itself on the poet and prevented him from expressing his emotions directly. He instead allowed his imagination to play on them and he expressed their poignancy in visions of what might have been had they found a less happy response. This is the secret of his love-poems.

It may be that a taste, growing ever stronger and stronger, for personal poetry, for poetry that is, as it were, but an impassioned diary, has led me to exaggerate the extent of this element in Browning, and its importance. I would not be taken as underrating the other side of him, the subtle intellect, the immense powers of observation and construction. But I do think that these were largely developed as a screen for a lyricist who was afraid of himself.

Oscar Wilde

A LITTLE while ago by way of celebrating the centenary of Byron's death, nearly every critic in England felt himself in honour bound to attempt to explain why that poet holds a higher place in Continental than in English estimation. It is a matter that has been canvassed again and again, and in the course of innumerable discussions some light, I think, has been thrown on the problem, which is one of the prettiest in all the theory of international literature. Byron was a great, and above all a typical figure : he did not so much invent Byronism as give it a name, and that because he was the first to isolate it in large and recognisable quantities from the confused emotional material of the age. His career was spectacular, and his end both spectacular and heroic. Moreover, what now makes us rank him somewhat lower than do Continental readers is something which is more apparent to us than to them, something which hides more from us than from them his none the less real virtues. The intolerable roughness and even shoddiness of his style are facts which do, for us, fight against his strength and originality : for foreigners, reading him whether in translation or in the original, they are necessarily facts of less weight.

Now the position of Oscar Wilde, here and abroad, has many points of similarity to this. We tend here more and more to look on him as a writer decidedly of the second rate. His influence, never very strong with the mature, grows less and less even with the young ; and undergraduates are ceasing to quote his epigrams in their essays. The time is perhaps coming when it will no longer be a hopeful enterprise to revive his plays. It would not be easy to find any critic of literature who would be likely to refer to him as a considerable writer. Nevertheless, even with us, his name conveys a vague sense as of something important, and abroad it does much more than that. In Germany, certainly, most critics would name Shakespeare, Byron and Wilde as the three writers whom England has given to the world.

Those who say this may make themselves seem a little absurd to us ; but what they state is a fact and not an opinion. In literature the persons whom a nation gives to the world are those whom the world consents to accept from her. We may continue to offer Shelley, Keats and Wordsworth as alternatives, but it is Byron that is chosen. We may offer as an alternative either George Meredith or Mr. Hardy, if we please, but it is Wilde that is chosen. This is a fact, and, instead of looking at it as though it were an inexplicable curiosity of nature, we shall do well to ask ourselves whether it does not spring from a fact of even greater interest, whether we must not in view of it apply to Wilde standards rather different from those applicable to writers who are ours alone, whether we should not attempt to see in him something more than simply an author of English prose and verse.

At first sight, the parallel with Byron does not appear likely to be very fruitful. Byron's virtues, we have said, are to some extent obscured from us by the roughness of his style. But, though Wilde may not have been—and I do not think that it can be maintained that he was—in the first rank of English prose-writers, yet smoothness, brilliance, and glitter of style are among the chief of his qualities. For the rest, a certain similarity of fate is obvious enough ; but Wilde's downfall and his wretched death in Paris make but a sordid caricature of Byron's mysterious exile from England and his heroic death in Greece.

When we consider Wilde, of course, the imagination is stirred by that sudden and disastrous reversal of fortune, by fate's evident rebuke to good luck too great and too insolently borne. He set out at an early period to make himself, with apparently small materials, a conspicuous figure, and when he fell, it was, for apparently small reason, in a blaze of conspicuousness. But such things do not happen quite accidentally, and their causes must be sought.

Let us, once and for all, be frank about his offence. It was a squalid and disgusting business, with every circumstance of vulgarity and some of madness. But the crime for which he was sentenced was not a great crime. It was one which goes oftener known and unpunished than any other ; and Wilde was not a great sinner, no Nero or Heliogabalus or Cæsar Borgia.

Yet he and the public at large were for the first time at one in holding that he was a great sinner. The crowds which howled savagely outside the Old Bailey after he had been found guilty and he himself writing *De Profundis* in Reading Gaol were in agreement that he was an enemy of society whom society had crushed. He says :—

" Of course I know that from one point of view things will be made different for me than for others; must indeed, by the very nature of the case, be made so. The poor thieves and outcasts who are imprisoned here with me are in many respects more fortunate than I am. The little way in grey city or green field that saw their sin is small ; to find those who know nothing of what they have done they need go no further than a bird might fly between the twilight and the dawn ; but for me the world is shrivelled to a handsbreadth, and everywhere I turn my name is written on the rocks in lead. For I have come, not from obscurity into the momentary notoriety of time, but from a sort of eternity of fame to a sort of eternity of infamy, and sometimes seem to myself to have shown, if indeed it required showing, that between the famous and the infamous there is but one step, if as much as one."

There is in this much of the megalomania which undoubtedly was one of the causes contributory to his disaster. It makes a peculiar contrast with the picture of Wilde, after his release, loafing outside the Café de la Paix, to invite the recognition and the curiosity and the free drinks of chance English tourists, one of whom, questioned as to whether anything had struck him about Wilde, replied : "Yes, he always wore tartan mittens." But in what I have quoted there is something more than megalomania. At the time, Wilde's fall reverberated hugely and the echoes of it have not really yet died away. He had, to be sure, enjoyed a very great reputation, as literary reputations go ; but it is not often that an English man of letters secures, by whatever means, such a place in the public imagination as this. The thing becomes more peculiar when we repeat that he was not a writer of the first rank or even of marked originality. This is, in short, the problem to be examined.

His first book of importance, the *Poems* of 1881, is in its way a peculiar collection. It is evidently the work of a man of much talent ; but it is exceedingly like a volume of serious parodies. Young poets imitate, they cannot as a rule help imitating, what they have admired. This is part of the stage of immaturity and does no harm. But one's first impression on reading these early pieces by Wilde is that a young man who could imitate so fluently, so copiously and so successfully the manners of so many different masters ought to be engaged in original work. He copies even Milton whom, however, he sees through a mist, as it were, of Wordsworth. This is the opening of his sonnet on the Bulgarian atrocities :—

> " Christ, dost thou live indeed ? or are thy bones
> Still straitened in their rock-hewn sepulchre ?
> And was thy Rising only dreamed by her
> Whose love of thee for all her sin atones ?
> For here the air is horrid with men's groans,
> The priests who call upon thy name are slain,
> Dost thou not hear the bitter wail of pain
> From those whose children lie upon the stones ? "

The very excellence of the thing—for of its kind it is excellent—almost takes one's breath away. As one goes on one finds more that is surprising. The combined manners of Keats, Morris and Swinburne come in very usefully to help a young man, who has absolutely nothing of his own to say, to three ornate narrative poems. There are ballads reminiscent of Swinburne and Rossetti. Andrew Lang's attempt to found an English Pléiade echoes here in a villanelle on Theocritus —of all poets in the world ! Contemporaries in

France have their share with *Impression du Matin* and other pieces. Tennyson too is laid under contribution ; and the best and simplest of the shorter poems is actually an echo of Tom Hood.

In the ordinary way there would be more malevolence than usefulness in such an analysis as this of the work of a young writer. But in the ordinary way the young writer, so long as he is thus copying his favourite models, is still plainly learning his job. By the time he has learnt how to imitate Swinburne or Keats, or whomever it may be, smoothly and successfully, he has ceased to wish to do anything of the kind. But for Wilde the styles of other poets were part of his material ; and he sometimes appropriates them with so persuasive an air of having the right to do it, that one is left at a loss to say whether the results are truly independent and his own or not.

In the shorter poems, this peculiarity is of little importance, for the poems themselves are of practically none. Wilde's reputation as a poet rests almost entirely on two pieces, both of which are derivative in style and yet both of which have a life of their own. *The Sphinx* gives its author's age as under twenty, which, to speak with frankness, I cannot bring myself to believe. It is much too remarkable an exercise in literary decoration for this to be possible, when one compares it with the other work of the same kind.

It *is* remarkable, and it *is* an exercise. But for Baudelaire and Swinburne it could never have been written. Cats and the fascination of sin, the names of precious stones and other " stunning " words, as Rossetti called them, a sinister disillusionment with life, and hints at strange vices—it is hard to say what in this is the contribution of the poet. Perhaps the form : for the stanza of *In Memoriam* undergoes a definite and interesting change when it is written as a couplet, with the rhymes concealed and not dwelt on. It takes on a different movement, very characteristic and rather impressive. This is, I fancy, Wilde's one invention in literary technique.

But so much will not explain the definite impression made on us that the poem is a valid work of art, and not to be dismissed as derivative or insincere, though both these faults could be shown in it. But what is to be made of such a passage as this ?—

" Or had you shameful secret guests and did you
hurry to your home
Some Nereid coiled in amber foam with curious
rock crystal breasts ?

Or did you treading through the froth call to
the brown Sidonian
For tidings of Leviathan, Leviathan or Behemoth ?

Or did you when the sun was set climb up the
cactus-covered slope
To meet your swarthy Ethiop whose body was
of polished jet ?

Or did you while the earthen skiffs dropped
down the grey nilotic flats
At twilight and the flickering bats flew round
the temple's triple glyphs

Steal to the border of the bar and swim across
the silent lake
And slink into the vault and make the Pyramid
your lupanar

Till from each black sarcophagus rose up the
painted swathed dead?
Or did you lure unto your bed the ivory-horned
Tragelaphos?

Or did you love the god of flies who plagued the
Hebrews and was splashed
With wine unto the waist? or Pasht, who had
green beryls for her eyes?

Or that young god, the Tyrian, who was more
amorous than the dove
Of Ashtaroth? or did you love the god of the
Assyrian,

Whose wings, like strange, transparent talc, rose
high above his hawk-faced head,
Painted with silver and with red and ribbed with
rods of Oreichalch?

Or did huge Apis from his car leap down and
lay before your feet
Big blossoms of the honey-sweet and honey-
coloured nenuphar?"

When the undergraduate (or so, at least, it used to be) reads this for the first time his heart leaps up, for he beholds what an immense amount of entertainment can be got of mere words. And one's instinct still is to say of *The Sphinx*: This is great fun. For it is entirely something, and it is equally certainly nothing on a higher level than that. The extravagance of the decoration is at once self-conscious and naïve. The ideas are mere counters, and the poem expresses no feeling, unless it be a delight in verbal and metrical virtuosity. But as such it exists and has an enduring spark of life in it.

The Ballad of Reading Gaol is a different matter. It was written later in Wilde's life, it describes an actual experience, and it is meant to convey a real feeling. But it too is derivative and its derivations are curious. One can understand that Wilde should again have taken something from Tom Hood for this purpose, but his borrowing from Coleridge is a good deal less easy to explain. Yet it is undoubtedly there :—

" They glided past, they glided fast,
    Like travellers through a mist :
They mocked the moon in a rigadoon
    Of delicate turn and twist.
And with formal pace and loathsome grace
    The phantoms kept their tryst.

With mop and mow, we saw them go,
    Slim shadows hand in hand :
About, about, in ghostly rout
    They trod a saraband :
And the damned grotesques made arabesques,
    Like the wind upon the sand ! "

This is as self-conscious in its decorative effect as are the passages in which Wilde remembers too suddenly and too clearly that he is describing a realistic modern tragedy :—

" The Governor was strong upon
    The Regulations Act :
The Doctor said that Death was but
    A scientific fact :
And twice a day the Chaplain called,
    And left a little tract."

How are we to reconcile these incongruities and the constant straining of feeling throughout the poem, as in the verses beginning " Yet each man kills the thing he loves," with the evident fact that it is a work of power and beauty ? Yet it makes a deep impression on almost all who read it, and very much the impression that Wilde intended, of a compassionate revolt against the cruelty of human justice. We can only say that a certain kind of insincerity was natural and essential in Wilde and, for the moment, leave it at that.

The reaching after effect which is the prime force of *The Sphinx* and the disfigurement of *The Ballad of Reading Gaol* is less disconcerting in his prose than in his verse. In prose it can, and very often does, take the form of wit, whereas in verse it takes too often the form of false emotion. And, in so far as Wilde's fame is based on his works at all, it is based on four or five works in prose, on *The Importance of Being Earnest* and *Lady Windermere's Fan*, on *De Profundis* and *Intentions* and *A House of Pomegranates* and *The Picture of Dorian Gray*.

It is here, it seems to me, that his genius, as expressed in his writings, is most often exaggerated. His habit of epigram, which makes a restless glitter over the surface of his plays and stories, can be paralleled from the novels of Disraeli, from whom too he derives his quite conscious and not all fatuous delight in aristocracy and opulence. Some of his sayings are acute and some are shallow ; but, as the conversational epigrammatist will, he contrives to make them all look exactly alike.

" I adore simple pleasures. They are the last refuge of the complex."

"No nice girl should ever waltz with such particularly younger sons! It looks so fast!"

"Better to take pleasure in a rose than to put its root under a microscope."

"Nothing is so dangerous as being too modern. One is apt to grow old-fashioned quite suddenly."

The prose of which such are the high lights is not of the first order, whether in style or in wisdom; and when he aims at beauty it cannot be said that he reaches a much higher level:—

"But, see, it is dawn already. Draw back the curtains and open the windows wide. How cool the morning air is! Piccadilly lies at our feet like a long riband of silver. A faint purple mist hangs over the Park, and the shadows of the white houses are purple. It is too late to sleep. Let us go down to Covent Garden and look at the roses. Come! I am tired of thought."

Let us then turn to the stories. The fairy-stories are charming; but will it be seriously maintained that they or *Lord Arthur Savile's Crime* are works of a high order? The stories in this second book are excellently ingenious and would be popular at any time and in almost any hands, but they are slight. A trivial thing may be a great work of art, if it displays a passionate delight in triviality; but these do not. And *The Picture of Dorian Gray* is disappointingly little more than ingenious. The idea is magnificent, even if it is a little too bizarre to be the vehicle for very intense feeling. The Preface is almost portentous, the most challenging and sweeping statement of the theory of art for art's sake ever made. But Wilde has sacrificed what might have been a masterpiece to his desire for immediate effect. Tussore silk curtains, opium-scented cigarettes, dressing-tables with large gold-topped bottles on them—these are the unhappy symbols, the first that came to hand, which Wilde employed for the embodiment of what after all was a vision of beauty. There is a book similar in spirit, by one of Wilde's favourite authors, which affords a fair comparison. It is verbose and ill-constructed, but it does to perfection what *Dorian Gray* fails to do. It is *Mademoiselle de Maupin* ; and the comparison is fatal to Wilde.

We proceed to the plays, his most successful works. These were written frankly for money ; but they are none the worse for that. Of their kind indeed they are very good. All his life he had treated the world as a theatre, and it required no great effort for him to submit himself to theatrical requirements. His stage effects are carried out with a gusto and sweep that made them exhilarating. Look at the curtain for the first act of *Lady Windermere's Fan* :—

"LADY WINDERMERE

Arthur, if that woman comes here—I warn you—

LORD WINDERMERE

Margaret, you'll ruin us !

LADY WINDERMERE

Us ! from this moment my life is separate from yours. But if you wish to avoid a public scandal, write at once to this woman and tell her I forbid her to come here !

LORD WINDERMERE

I will not—I cannot—she must come !

Lady Windermere

Then I shall do exactly as I have said. (*Goes R.*) You leave me no choice. (*Exit R.*)

Lord Windermere

(*Calling after her.*) Margaret ! Margaret ! (*A pause.*) My God ! What shall I do ? I dare not tell her who this woman really is. The shame would kill her. (*Sinks down into a chair and buries his face in his hands.*)"

One asks oneself involuntarily whether Wilde here has his tongue in his cheek or not. The scene is theatrical in the last degree, but effectively, magnificently theatrical. And the same may be said of the dialogue which was the element distinguishing his from the other " well made " plays of the time. His dialogue is fine of its sort, and, considering that it exists only for its own sake, it is introduced very deftly so as not to give any impression that it retards the action of the play. But it is not dramatic prose of the highest order. It stands to Congreve's prose, for example, just as the scene I have quoted stands to the knocking at the gate in *Macbeth*.

Wilde's plays, if the distinction be permissible, have theatrical rather than dramatic qualities. They exist for effect, not for expression—all, that is to say, except one of them, *The Importance of Being Earnest*. This admirable piece does express something of the author and something which one would hardly have expected to find in him—a simple and light-hearted sense of fun. It is more genuine than the other plays, and will probably outlive them all. But, delightful as it is, it is not a great masterpiece even of its own sort. One has of it an impression of, as it were, the *beauté du diable.* Its charm lies in its youthfulness, its freshness and liveliness. It has a good complexion and pleasant manners, but fine features are wanting.

From this analysis, I have omitted *Salome*, which is, perhaps, taking the whole world together, Wilde's most famous work, a fact not wholly due to Dr. Strauss's use of it as a libretto. It ranks, I think, somewhere with *The Sphinx* and with *Dorian Gray.* The idea is magnificently unexpected ; but the execution is only superficial. From the elements of sin and blasphemy which it contains Wilde has made a very striking stage-picture but he has done no more. It is, however, a very characteristic work.

From this brief and rapid examination, I emerge with the verdict that Wilde was a derivative and artificial writer. He aimed constantly at effect rather than at expressing something genuine in himself. He took always the shortest and easiest way to an effect. Not one of his works but has in it the obvious seeds of decay. Yet the figure of Wilde survives ; and it seems not unlikely that his legend will preserve some of his writings perhaps beyond their natural span of life.

The explanation is, I think, supplied by himself in *De Profundis* :—

" I was a man who stood in symbolic relations to the art and culture of my age. I had realised this for myself at the very dawn of my manhood, and had forced my age to realise it afterwards. Few men hold such a position in their own lifetime, and have it so acknowledged. It is usually discerned, if discerned at all, by the historian, or the critic long after both the man and his age have passed away. With me it was different. I felt it myself, and made others feel it. Byron was a symbolic figure, but his relations were to the passion of his age and its weariness of passion. Mine were to something more noble, more permanent, of more vital issue, of larger scope."

The parallel is unfortunate, for what Byron stood for was something decidedly stronger and more vital. But, like him, Wilde was a symbolic figure.

The origin of the movement he represented is not very easy to discover. It sprang perhaps from a revolt of part of the human race against a fate which seemed to be overtaking the whole. In the middle of the nineteenth century the wave of material improvement spread over the world and ugliness and narrowness came in its train. All the countries of Europe, one after another, were given up to industry, railways cut through their fields and the smoke of factory chimneys darkened their skies. Vast mean and degraded populations sprang up which had no songs nor any joy in life. The middle class, the mercantile code of life ruled everywhere ; and at once the artist sprang up in passionate reaction.

The reaction took different forms. Ruskin preached that pictures should have a religious effect on those who saw them. Morris, between his day-dreams, laboured for the abandonment of machinery. Poets in France retired to ivory towers and ululated more or less distinctly from the top windows. And soon the rebels began to make themselves deliberately as unlike their enemies as they could. The middle classes applauded virtue, therefore vice was to be exalted. The middle classes preached thrift, therefore waste was to be practised. The middle classes thought art should be instructive, therefore all art was to be perfectly useless. And Baudelaire smoked opium and Verlaine alternated hysterically between religion and wickedness and Gérard de Nerval trailed a lobster after him through the streets of Paris.

The movement became extravagant and was doomed not to persist as it had begun, for it was approaching the evil in an unhelpful manner. But while it lasted it was a very real thing. And into it came Wilde, a young man not at all hysterical, with many talents and in particular a very great talent for histrionics. So he made himself the centre and symbol of all that great and bizarre crusade against bourgeois ideas and morality.

He was not an originator, he was, much as he would have disliked the designation, a populariser. He summarised in his work what was then called *fin de siècle* art, and made it easy for the great public to understand. Almost every aspect of the movement was there. The sensualism of Baudelaire and his hinting at strange vices, Gautier's disinterested unmoral adoration of things that were hard, bright and sharp-edged, Verlaine's religiosity—all these with dashes of Satanism and cruelty and just so much of the doctrines of Ruskin and Morris as could be made to fit in with the rest without too startling an incongruity. One might almost say that Wilde was not so much a writer as a museum.

It is not to be said that this view disposes of him either as a legend or as a writer ; but it does, I think, explain him. He was artificial and insincere ; but there was something genuine in his artificiality and something vital in his insincerity. These were his main qualities, and in both of them he was at heart consistent. He held up his mind as a mirror to a whole side of the life of his time, and in that mirror there may still be seen a wonderfully varied and interesting picture.

So, he having made himself the compendium of this movement, mankind treated him as its leader and turned and crushed him ; and his name was removed from playbills and the crowds howled round the Old Bailey on learning that he had been sent to prison. He graciously gave the Decadence one head ; and humanity with a brutal but sure instinct promptly cut it off. Life took the opportunity to affirm that art shall not be permitted to declare itself independent of life. For the reverse of his own parallel between himself and Byron is what is true. Byron, by whatever means, proclaimed the revolt of life, passionate, energetic, indignant life, against a world which was unworthy of it. The movement at the head of which Wilde, with incomparable but characteristic arrogance, placed himself was, though I have called it a revolt, not so much that as an attempt at a secession. The Decadents did not contemplate the conquest of the world for better and nobler ideas. They stated their own superiority and contemptuously stepped aside. It was enough for them to make from time to time wounding remarks on the gross, struggling body of humanity which they had left behind them.

Now the Decadence was doomed to failure, whether it had received this wounding blow in the person of Wilde or not ; and it does not rank very high among the movements which in the course of history have at one time and another swept over Europe. But it had in it some of the finest and acutest, if not some of the strongest, spirits of the time. Its achievement was incomplete, fragmentary, unhappy ; but it achieved something. And a man who could make himself seem the typical figure of that movement and that achievement is not a man to be neglected.

Wilde, to be sure, deceived himself here as elsewhere. There was probably no really decadent strain in his nature. When, in *Dorian Gray*, he had to suggest abysmal wickedness he failed lamentably to make concrete the vague conception, and his attitude to the conception was all that could be desired from the severest of moralists. What distinguished him was the wax-like character of his mind which received a clear and readable impression of the main elements of his epoch. This process of assimilation and simplification made him a leading figure and then a legend ; and the legend, as I have said, will very likely make some of his works live longer than would otherwise be natural for them. But the man will always be more important than any of his works ; and it will be a long time, I think, before he disappears altogether from memory.